Working with design clients:
Tools and advice for successful partnerships

MEAGHAN DEE AND JESSICA MEHARRY

WITH CHAPTER 3 WRITTEN BY NAJLA MOUCHREK

BLOOMSBURY VISUAL ARTS
LONDON • NEW YORK • OXFORD • NEW DELHI • SYDNEY

BLOOMSBURY VISUAL ARTS
Bloomsbury Publishing Plc
50 Bedford Square, London, WC1B 3DP, UK
1385 Broadway, New York, NY 10018, USA
29 Earlsfort Terrace, Dublin 2, Ireland

BLOOMSBURY, BLOOMSBURY VISUAL ARTS
and the Diana logo are trademarks of Bloomsbury Publishing Plc

First published in Great Britain 2024

Copyright © Jessica Meharry and Meaghan Dee, 2024

For legal purposes the Image credits on p.224 constitute an extension of this copyright page.

Cover design: Meaghan Dee

All rights reserved. No part of this publication may be reproduced or transmitted in any form or by any means, electronic or mechanical, including photocopying, recording, or any information storage or retrieval system, without prior permission in writing from the publishers.

Bloomsbury Publishing Plc does not have any control over, or responsibility for, any third-party websites referred to or in this book. All internet addresses given in this book were correct at the time of going to press. The author and publisher regret any inconvenience caused if addresses have changed or sites have ceased to exist, but can accept no responsibility for any such changes.

A catalogue record for this book is available from the British Library.
A catalog record for this book is available from the Library of Congress.

Working with design clients: Tools and advice for successful partnerships
was authored by Meaghan Dee and Jessica Meharry,
with Chapter 3 written by Najla Mouchrek.

ISBN: HB: 978-1-3503-5883-6
PB: 978-1-3503-5882-9
ePDF: 978-13503-5884-3
eBook: 978-1-3503-5885-0

Typeset by Meaghan Dee
Printed and bound in India

To find out more about our authors and books visit www.bloomsbury.com and sign up for our newsletters.

Acknowledgments

This book would not be possible without the contributions from other design educators, students, and researchers. In the early days of our research, the *AIGA Design Educators Community* (DEC) facilitated this project by hosting numerous events about student-run design studios. These events connected us with other educators and created support and community.

During her time on the DEC board, Meaghan found some of the greatest supporters, collaborators, mentors, and friends she could hope for. Additionally during that time, Meaghan, Anne H. Berry, Penina Laker, Rebecca Tegtmeyer, and Kelly Walters co-created (with the DEC) the following pledge for design educators: "I commit to being anti-racist, to upholding all design histories, to distributing knowledge, to demonstrating impact, to creating culture, and to supporting student life experiences." She hopes all educators can reflect on their own values and infuse them into their classes.

We also want to share our heartfelt gratitude to *Design Incubation* an organization that hosted a transformational writing fellowship (now run by *Writing Space*). Before, during, and after our participation in the fellowship program, Aaris Sherin and Robin Landa gave us advice, feedback, and encouragement. They also de-mystified the writing process and helped us break this project into manageable pieces. We remain overwhelmed by their kindness and generosity.

Jessica would like to thank Meaghan for continually reaching out to initiate this project and keep it going to the finish line. I would also like to thank all of my colleagues at Columbia College Chicago and IIT Institute of Design who supported me through these past few years. Finally, I am infintely grateful for my partner, Ames, for their boundless love, guidance, patience, and wisdom.

Meaghan would like to thank Jessica for being an incredible collaborator. Thanks to Helen Armstrong, David Hisaya Asari, Anne H. Berry, Meena Khalili, Marty Maxwell Lane, Alberto Rigau, Kaleena Sales, Rebecca Tegtmeyer, and Kelly Walters for always answering my questions and inspiring me through your own writing and research. I'm also grateful to my colleagues at Virginia Tech. Special thanks to my husband, Nick, for supporting my efforts and seeing the value in what I do. And love to our daughter, Finial, for reminding us what is important beyond work and for bringing us so much joy. Also love to our dog, Dexter; I miss you.

Lastly, we want to thank all of our students. We have learned so much from you. This book is for you.

4 TABLE OF CONTENTS

Acknowledgements p.3
Introduction p.6

PART 1

Why?

PART 2

What?

CHAPTER 1

Learning through experience 14

CHAPTER 2

Connecting to industry & community 26

CHAPTER 3

Becoming empowered 42
Chapter written by
Najla Mouchrek

CHAPTER 4

Engaging with communities 62

CHAPTER 5

Finding focus & targeting clients 82

CHAPTER 6

Achieving learning goals 96

TABLE OF CONTENTS 5

PART 3

Who?

PART 4

How?

CHAPTER 7

Exploring work roles 112

CHAPTER 8

Establishing relationships 134

CHAPTER 9

Sustaining relationships 152

CHAPTER 10

Launching a studio 162

CHAPTER 11

Managing the money 178

CHAPTER 12

Planning for the future 198

PART 4 IS FOCUSED ON
THE MANAGEMENT AND
STRATEGIC PLANNING
OF FULL-FLEDGED
STUDENT-RUN STUDIOS.

Conclusion p.210
Index p.220
Image credits p.224

APPLIED ADVICE

Design Streak Studio students at work with their faculty Creative and Art Director, Archana Shekara.
Photo credit: Lyndsie Schlick

Introduction

Real-world experience

We learn to design by **doing** design. That's what design is—using ideas to bring something into the world. Or as design researcher Herbert Simon put it, to design is to "devise courses of action aimed at changing existing situations into preferred ones." So the question becomes, what kind of **doing** helps us learn how to design? We—design educators—incorporate many different kinds of doing depending on where you—design students—are in your program. As a beginning student, you explore doing design in studio classes, often starting with formal exercises to help you understand and master technical skills. Later in your program, you shift to experiential learning, collaborating on full-fledged design projects, often with external clients or partners. It's that kind of learning that we're focusing on in this book.

Learning is most impactful when tied to real-world projects, which can serve as a gateway to professional practice. That's why working with communities and clients while in the safety of the classroom can be an excellent way to gain early experience. Getting started on client work can be tremendously challenging—but we're here to help! Throughout this book, we will share advice on everything from working with community partners and external clients, all the way to establishing a fully-operational student-run design studio. We will tackle the why, what, who, and how of client work in the design classroom, while sharing interviews and case studies from both faculty and students.

1. Simon, Herbert Alexander. 2008. *The Sciences of the Artificial*. Third edition. Cambridge, MA: MIT Press.

Who we are

Meaghan spent her first three years at Virginia Tech as the director of a student-run, faculty-led graphic design agency. She was essentially thrown into the deep end, jumping straight into running a fully operational studio with large-scale projects already underway. While systems were already in place, no one was available to train her on daily operations, so much of what she learned came from trial and error. She wished she'd had a guidebook available to help her during this time.

At the same time, Jessica was interested in creating a student-run design studio where she worked at Columbia College Chicago. She looked for guidance and advice in books and articles, but she couldn't find much. So, she applied for and received a Faculty Research Grant from the AIGA Design Educators Community (DEC) to research what faculty members were already doing that was working well. Her goal was to share those findings in conference presentations and in an article and then begin the work of starting a studio.

As luck would have it, Meaghan was serving on the AIGA DEC board and saw Jessica's research. It's the typical story of how networking goes—"Hey, I'm interested in this, and you're interested in this. Let's do something together!" And here we are.

Who is this book for?

We wrote this book with students in mind, but many audiences can benefit from our research and advice:

Students: This book is a behind-the-scenes look at what it takes to tackle client work inside (and outside) the design classroom. Whether you're assuming a leadership position at your institution or just starting with your first client project, we wrote this book for you.

Faculty: This is the book we, the authors, wish we had when we were taking over a student-run design studio (Meaghan) and considering starting one (Jessica). We hope that this can help serve as a guide for any stage—from dreaming to revisioning.

Administrators: Working with clients and communities is complex and requires a lot of effort and planning. This book provides insights and can help you better understand what support might be needed and the benefits these endeavors can have for your institution.

Founders of design studios: While we center our work on examples in the classroom, many of the strategies and principles apply to establishing design studios outside the academy.

Why did we write this book?

Real-world client work is one of the most valuable activities students can engage in before graduation. It is an opportunity to see what it is really like to work as a designer and to practice adapting to unexpected hurdles. With the right mindset and mentorship, this work can set the foundation for empowerment and community connection.

There are hundreds of faculty-led, student-run graphic design and marketing agencies in the United States and around the world. Additionally, many more universities and institutions are working to establish new firms in these subject areas, and in emerging creative technologies such as augmented reality (AR), virtual reality (VR), and artificial intelligence (AI). Existing student-run firms face many challenges, including high student and faculty turnover, managing clients and budgets, and lack of administrative support. As a result, these studios are often just hanging on by a thread. This book provides faculty managers and students with the expertise and guidance needed to thrive. While many programs don't have the infrastructure or size to handle a full-fledged studio, students can still benefit from working with design clients. Whether integrating one client project in a course, dedicating an entire semester to working with community partners, or building a standalone studio, we will provide insight and practical tips for success.

This book will examine client work and design studios in the larger context of design education. Many faculty members who oversee client projects and design agencies get so caught up in daily fires and keeping the organization afloat that they don't have time to think about educational best practices and the relationship to broader curricula. We will offer guidance for managing studios and for helping to prepare for a complex future. We will also supply resources to aid student success. Throughout this book, we will provide:

1. **Methods** for integrating best teaching and learning practices into classroom-based client work (and student design studios) and methods for how to get the most out of experiential education opportunities.
2. **Advice** on how to launch, operate, and grow a student-run design firm and how to work with clients in the context of the design classroom.
3. **Resources** and tangible takeaways for students and educators, including sample timesheets, estimates, invoices, and evaluation forms.
4. **Support** for awareness, reflection, and self-care during a journey of empowerment throughout one's education.

Real-world experience

Educators strive to model the academic experience after the real-world practices of collaboration, client service, and design methodology. In the studio, students "learn by doing," and practicums/studios are an ideal vehicle for teaching *how to design* and *how to pitch* work. Students learn from practice, actively working on projects and advancing through that process rather than solely by applying theory or style. In addition, many researchers and educators have found using "live" clients most beneficial. We've also heard directly from many employers how much the client experience makes students stand out from their peers.

Challenging but rewarding

While there are tremendous benefits to integrating client work and student studios into design programs, we won't sugar-coat it—there are also incredible challenges. Project managers must worry about funding, resources, institutional support (or lack thereof), hiring and training students, and dealing with clients—just to name a few concerns. But our hope is that sharing experiences and expertise from those who have been working this way for years can help make it easier to navigate whatever might lie ahead.

FIGURE 0.1

Virginia Tech students Rachael Quan and Sydney Johnson participating in the design sprint, DesignUP.

How to use this book

Our primary audience for this book is our students, so we will write to "you." At the same time, all of the information will be valuable to your instructors, so we include faculty perspectives on how to work with design clients in the classroom.

This book is divided into four sections:

1. Why?

The first section, *Why?*, explains the benefits of client work in the design classroom. The section situates classroom-based client work into the broader context of design education, and demonstrates how this education can best prepare students for industry. *Why?* also details how experiential education can be a path to empowerment for students.

2. What?

The second section, *What?*, focuses on the experiential work opportunities that are available—from engaging with communities, to working with clients. *What?* also details how you can structure client work within different programs and curricular requirements.

3. Who?

The third section, *Who?*, identifies who will be conducting the design work—students and their roles—and who they will be working with—clients. *Who?* also gives advice for getting stakeholder buy-in, such as how to sell the idea of client work in the design classroom to administrators or financial gatekeepers.

4. How?

The book's last section, *How?*, specifically focuses on the management and strategic planning of full-fledged student-run studios. This section is geared toward those considering starting an agency, taking over an agency, or planning the future development of an existing agency.

Part one

Why?

CHAPTER 1

Learning through experience

CHAPTER 2

Connecting to industry & community

CHAPTER 3

Becoming empowered

HOW?
WHO?
WHAT?
WHY?

BRAINSTORMING

Virginia Tech students Grace Cheung and Emily Dinh develop client ideas during the design sprint, DesignUP.

Chapter 1

Learning through experience

One goal of design education is to be a gateway to professional practice. When working with clients, you learn through action by working on projects and advancing through that process, rather than solely applying theory in a classroom.

This chapter situates client work in the design classroom within a larger educational context, by addressing learning-through-doing, project outcomes, and a variety of management and learning styles. We connect these approaches to the well-established tradition of experiential education.

HOW?

WHO?

WHAT?

WHY?

Problem-solving by design

The word *design* can mean different things. It is used as a *verb* when we refer to the process of design. For example, "I am designing this website." Design is a *noun* when we refer to the designed object, as in, "This is my logo design." We also use design as an *adjective* when we describe a design-oriented approach to something, such as design thinking, design methodology, or design management. Taken even further, we also refer to the field of design—all of the different disciplines and crafts that use design as a problem-solving process.

No matter how we use the word design, all these meanings share the fact that design (as a field) is a service industry. Designers usually work in service for someone else, such as clients, community partners, customers, or end users. For example, a potential client or partner seeks the services of a designer to help them do something for their business or organization, such as designing a logo and a brand identity, developing an advertising campaign, or strategizing an outreach program. They turn to designers for expertise

> "**Working on real-world projects taught me to ask better questions. In traditional design studio classes, you only rely on your own preferences and good design principles. With real-world projects, there is a whole other set of opinions you need to cater to. In order to meet the expectations of clients, I had to learn how to dig deep and get to the "why" behind every project."**
>
> —Micah Vetter, *alumnus of Design Streak at Illinois State University*

and problem-solving approaches that they—the client or partner—don't have. Designers then seek to add value for the client by understanding their needs and interests so that they can transform those challenges into thoughtful, responsible, and successful design solutions. How we develop relationships and practices with these clients and partners is critical to success—for both them and us.

This book is about how students and faculty can develop these complex, successful client relationships within a design classroom or program context. These kinds of experiences move beyond abstract, theoretical design exercises to allow you to engage with an existing challenge in the world. There's a lot to learn, and it's not always easy. But it's always rewarding. So let's get started!

Class doesn't officially start until 9am, but the studio is already bustling with activity by 8:30am. One student team is finalizing its presentation for a client meeting later that morning. Another team is preparing to head out and conduct field research, including ethnographic observations of a shopping center, and interviews with customers. The instructor is providing feedback to a third team on some concepts the students developed the night before. After a quick critique, the instructor will check in with the field team to see if they have any questions before leaving. The instructor will then respond to a couple of emails from potential clients, before finally sitting down with the client meeting team at 9am to practice their presentation.

Learning through doing

Many design education programs aim to provide you—design students—with a "passport to practice."[1] **Educators want you to be able to learn about design by actually doing design**, an approach called "learning by doing," in which instructors assign real-world client projects. In individual courses and stand-alone student-run design studios, you actively work on design projects and advance those through iterative processes rather than solely by learning theory. The idea is that you learn through action when working on real-world projects.

To create these experiences, design educators establish connections between external organizations and industries and their universities. In many cases, these projects involve simulation of a workplace environment in which you take on professional roles (such as art director, project manager, and social media lead) and follow procedures identical to those used in design practice. This simulation—sometimes called a practicum—helps model the industry practices of collaboration, innovation, client service, and design methodology. The studio space allows you to create the "habits of mind" necessary to enter the profession.[2] Additionally, **the unexpected challenges of a studio lay the groundwork for an adaptable mindset.**

The practices within these projects and studios vary widely in teaching styles, curriculum requirements, faculty involvement, student autonomy, client selection, client interaction, institutional support, and facilities. By identifying the goals of design education, faculty and students can better structure these experiences to achieve those aims. For example, in these environments, you are typically not taught, you are coached. The coach's role is to demonstrate, advise, question, and criticize. To make this practicum a meaningful learning experience, you and your instructor must engage in "reflection-in-action."[3] Through this interaction, you can begin teaching yourself and learning from your instructors.

Developing and managing client work in the classroom and in student-run campus design studios is hard work for both faculty and students. It takes more time, energy, and commitment than teaching and learning within a traditional studio class. Faculty are continually caught up in the daily management tasks of keeping their students, clients, and projects on track. Meanwhile, you learn as you go, balancing real-world expectations and pressures with your other coursework. **The challenges are many, but the rewards are even greater.**

ACTIVITY 1.1

Questions for internal reflection[4]

Reflecting on your own design process can also be thought of as metacognition, *or thinking about your own thinking. When you better understand your own thinking processes, you become more skilled at developing a range of creative strategies and ideas for the designs you are working on. Metacognition also helps you understand how your thinking processes might differ from those of a fellow student or collaborator. When everyone collaborating in a group starts to be aware of these differences, you can develop even more diverse and creative ideas.*

Here are a few questions that can prompt metacognitive reflection. Try keeping an ongoing journal and answer these questions for every project you work on, even solo projects.

- How did you approach your design task?
  What strategies did you use to solve your design problem?
- Did you have a clear understanding of the problem?
  If not, how did you gain more understanding along the way?
- What information and research influenced your design and why?
  How did you go about finding it?
- Did you use any specific creative strategy that you think was successful?
- Did any of your collaborators use strategies that you think were successful?
- Did you execute your design task differently from what you are used to?
- How much time did you spend on the project?
  Was that the amount of time you anticipated?
- What would you do differently next time?

Learning through experience

Another way of thinking about learning by doing in design education is through the lens of experiential education. The Association for Experiential Education defines experiential education as "a philosophy that informs many methodologies in which educators purposefully engage with learners in direct experience and focused reflection in order to increase knowledge, develop skills, clarify values, and develop people's capacity to contribute to their communities."[5] Experiential educational practices are proven to impact students positively.

Experiential learning links education, work, and personal development by offering a framework to understand the critical connections between learning objectives and "real world" activities.[6] Learning is a holistic adaptive process that can provide conceptual bridges across life situations. Perhaps most importantly, **research shows that you are more likely to get a job when you participate in practicum and internship-type experiences,** all of which fall under the umbrella of work-based learning (WBL). Experiential learning manifests itself in the design classroom in many ways, including:

- **Project**-based learning (inquiry-based, problem-based, practitioner-focused)
- **Community**-based learning (service projects, place-based curriculum, off-campus study)
- **Integrative learning** (work-integrations, co-curricular integrations)
- **Internships and externships**
- **Active learning** (cooperative and collaborative, game-based, case studies).

Client-based practicum experiences in design education could be a combination of all of the examples listed, but are primarily focused on project-based learning. Some specific types of project-based learning in design programs (with examples from this book) include:

- Collaborative assignments
- Community-based learning
- Capstone courses and projects
- Practicums
- Student-run design studios.

These high-impact practices include integrative and applied learning in which you synthesize information across disciplines. The nature of these activities dictates regular interaction with your instructor and peers, giving you feedback that is often almost continuous. As many of these design practicum courses are often capstone courses, they are culminating moments in which you can integrate and apply what you have learned throughout your studies.

It's also important to recognize that not everyone has had the same academic preparation prior to college. People come from very different backgrounds and experiences. The best instructors teach with this in mind, meeting you where you are. When managed well, learning through experience leads to more equitable outcomes because it helps even the "playing field." You are coached through these experiences in ways that you don't always get coached in a traditional classroom. You can make direct connections between what you're learning and how you'll use that knowledge on the job. In addition, students from diverse backgrounds are coached

---

MINI-ACTIVITY

Co-create a code-of-conduct or values statement with your classmates

COMMUNICATING CARE DURING EXPERIENTIAL EDUCATION

Syllabus statements from faculty

Rebecca Tegtmeyer
Associate Professor, Michigan State University
While I am not a trained mental health professional, I am someone you can reach out to if you're struggling, whether or not your concerns pertain directly to this course. Our conversations will be confidential, though please remember that all faculty are mandatory reporters if issues of violence, sexual harm, or harassment are disclosed. I do ask that if you are having any personal difficulties (that are affecting your participation) please notify me sooner than later so we can discuss options for you to move forward. I'm a good listener, and I can help connect you to campus and other resources that are here to help you. As your course instructor, I am committed to helping you successfully complete this course, but it's even more important to me that you experience our classroom as a space that is open, inclusive, and supportive. I am a mom and a commuter, I do my best to make it on-time for class, however, situations do arise. I will try to notify you all sooner than later if I will be late to class.

Meaghan Dee
Associate Professor, Virginia Tech
Students in this class are encouraged to speak up and participate during class meetings. The class will represent a diversity of individual beliefs, backgrounds, and experiences—and every member of this class must show respect for every other member of this class. Additionally, if you have a preferred name or pronoun, please let me and your classmates know. And please do not hesitate to correct me if I make a mistake. My preferred pronouns are *she* and *her*. All are welcome here.

Penina Laker (*co-created with her class*)
Associate Professor, Washington University
We are committed to the ongoing work of anti-racism and we ask you to do the same. To move forward, we must acknowledge the role that designers have contributed to the creation and perpetuation of unjust systems and institutions. We also realize that this work takes time and sustained involvement; let us all work together and approach new knowledge with a learning mindset.

---

through these work-based experiences, which offers them opportunities to "see" themselves in the profession.

In all these ways, experiential education is immersive, purposeful, social, and builds relationships between students and faculty members. Teachers become curators of experience, providing a large amount of feedback. In return, you gain a sense of ownership over your work, and become a co-constructor of your learning.

A model for empowerment

Current research builds on previous experiential learning research on personal development, to focus on students' co-construction of learning, leading to empowerment. For example, Najla Mouchrek co-created, in collaboration with Mark Benson, the "Theory of Integrated Empowerment in the Transition to Adulthood."[7] In this model, four catalysts—agency, purpose, mentoring, and community—lead young adults to become self-directed and to find a meaningful role within society. Najla says, **"Empowerment emerges through real-world experimentation and active engagement in relevant activities, integrated through self-reflection and meaning-making."** Najla discusses this model of empowerment at greater length in *Chapter 3: Becoming empowered*.

To be comfortable being creative, you must first feel safe, welcome, and worthy. As such, every classroom should be free from discrimination and prejudice. Design faculty members take on many different roles (such as coach, mentor, educator, and advisor), yet one of their most important "unofficial" responsibilities is to be an advocate. Faculty should affirm the inherent dignity of all of their students, recognizing that each individual has unique circumstances and challenges. Faculty can communicate this verbally and in syllabi and learning management systems (see the previous page for examples). Students can find a sense of agency and purpose by having industry success—such as bringing a client project to fruition—and being acknowledged for their small and large achievements.

ARCS OF TIME

Example from Renée Walker's Auto-ethnography Typographic Timeline project.

ACTIVITY 1.2

Auto-ethnography typographic timeline[8]

In this exercise, instructor Renée Walker asks students to view their personal experiences through a typographic lens. Students collect and reflect upon typographic imagery that is personally meaningful for them.

INSTRUCTIONS:
Collect and gather a minimum of eight images using a provided template.
Provide caption information with the following:
- Date created
- Creator (if known)
- Artifact title
- Artifact type
- Location (where was it made or found)
- Description (1–3 sentences)
- Citation of source

During class, students then work together to organize their captioned images in a timeline form. The y-axis is organized by time, and the x-axis by category (i.e. formal properties, artifact type, etc.). Students use strings to make connections between each others' years and categories to create a non-linear timeline of their type samples.

Source: *teachingresource.aiga.org/project/autoethnography-typographic-timeline*

Engaging with ethics and equity

MINI-ACTIVITY

Take a moment and reflect on what "good design" means to you.

Are you purely thinking about aesthetics? Does what you're exposed to influence your visual preference?

Does content impact whether a design is "good" or not?

Designers work with other people. In those interactions, you will inevitably encounter issues related to ethics, power (and who does or doesn't have it), and equity. **Will your design solutions help or harm an individual or a community? How do you know?** To tackle these questions, designers need to know themselves, their clients, and the contexts and communities in which they're working. We talk about this in detail in *Chapter 4*.

One reflective approach is auto-ethnography, a tool that Gaby Hernández, Associate Professor at the University of Arkansas, uses for self-discovery and sense-making for designers about their own identity. This process informs future interactions with others. Gaby asks students to explore their identity, background, and personal history. Then, they create design projects that manifest their findings. (You can read more about Gaby in *Chapter 4*.) Renée Walker, Associate Professor at Thomas Jefferson University, uses another approach to auto-ethnography that focuses on typography and personal history (see *Activity 1.2* on the previous spread).

Building on this foundation of self-awareness and reflective practice, designers must consciously examine their ethics and actions. But what exactly do we mean by ethics? Designer and educator Juliette Cezzar says that being ethical often means "not participating in something you don't believe in, or not doing something that you know will cause harm to others."[9] Other designers have thought about ethics so deeply that they've created their own approaches, such as Laura Javier's "The Designer's 10-point Hippocratic Oath."[10]

Actively thinking about ethical issues when you don't have an immediate problem (aka "a fire to put out") will help you react appropriately when problems arise. For example, sometimes designers feel uncomfortable with having to stand up to a client when they make an inappropriate comment or ask for a piece that goes against the designer's beliefs. Power dynamics are also complicated by the teacher–student relationship in the classroom. Experiential education is an excellent way to practice dealing with issues within the constraints and relative safety of the classroom environment.

Conclusion

Students who participate in experiential education become less prejudiced and more empathetic to bias and injustice.[11]

In summary, one of the goals of design education is to guide you through learning by doing and learning through experience so that you become empowered to transition to professional design practice. This involves learning to deal with tricky ethical issues while working collaboratively with diverse people. In the following chapters, we will highlight examples of how students, faculty, and administrators can successfully engage in client-based and community partner projects in design classes.

Chapter 1 key concepts

auto-ethnography: autobiographical writing and reflection based on the lived experience of the author that connects one's personal insights to broader cultural, political, and social systems

equity: when everyone has what they need to succeed. Some people might need different kinds of access and support than others in order to achieve the same goals

ethics: morals or principles that guide your behavior and actions

metacognition: thinking about your thinking

practicum: the practical (applied) part of a course of study; putting theory or ideas into action

References

1. Tovey, Mike. 2015. *Design Pedagogy: Developments in Art and Design Education.* New York: Routledge.
2. Shulman, Lee S. "Signature pedagogies in the professions." *Daedalus* 134, no. 3 (2005): 52-59.
3. Schön, Donald A. 1987. *Educating the Reflective Practitioner: Toward a New Design for Teaching and Learning in the Professions.* San Francisco: Jossey-Bass.
4. Questions adapted from Hargrove, Ryan. 2012. "Fostering Creativity in the Design Studio: A Framework towards Effective Pedagogical Practices." *Art, Design & Communication in Higher Education* 10 (1): 7–31; and Kavousi, Shabnam, Patrick A. Miller, and Patricia A. Alexander. 2020. "Modeling Metacognition in Design Thinking and Design Making." *International Journal of Technology and Design Education* 30 (4): 709–35.
5. Association for Experiential Education. n.d. "What is Experiential Education?" aee.org/what-is-experiential-education.
6. Roberts, Jay W. 2015. *Experiential Education in the College Context: What It Is, How It Works, and Why It Matters.* New York: Routledge.
7. Mouchrek, N., & Benson, M. (2023). *The Theory of Integrated Empowerment in the Transition to Adulthood: Concepts and Measures. Frontiers in Sociology*, 8, 62.
8. "Design Teaching Resource." n.d. teachingresource.aiga.org.
9. Cezzar, Juliette. 2018. *The AIGA Guide to Careers in Graphic and Communication Design.* New York: Bloomsbury Academic.
10. Javier, Laura. n.d. "The Designer's 10-Point Hippocratic Oath." Laura Javier. designersoath.com/index.html.
11. Simons, Lori, Lawrence Fehr, Nancy Blank, Heather Connell, Denise Georganas, David Fernandez, and Verda Peterson. 2012. "Lessons Learned from Experiential Learning: What Do Students Learn from a Practicum/Internship?" *International Journal of Teaching and Learning in Higher Education* 24 (3): 325–34.

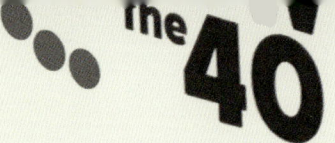

Only 40% of eligible US voters participated in the last midterm election. There are many reasons someone might choose not to vote.

"I don't have time to vote"
"I don't want to do the research"
"I don't care about the candidates"
"My voice doesn't matter"

If you have ever had any of these t[houghts] then you may have been part of the [60%] people who did not vote. Help us gro[w from] 40% and leave your stamp on demo[cracy]

— CSU G[raphic De]sign St[udents]

INTERACTIVE ENGAGEMENT

Students build an interactive gallery installation to promote voter engagement in Sarah Rutherford's Graphic Design for Social and Cultural Contexts class at Cleveland State University.

Chapter 2

Connecting to industry & community

We've established that one of the purposes of design education is to help prepare students to become professional designers. Whether that means you're going to work for a big, mainstream design firm or a small, nonprofit organization, design educators strive to keep their design programs connected to what's happening in the "real world." Educators are aware of what employers are looking for when hiring designers, and they structure client-based projects to help you prepare for those expectations.

In this chapter, we'll discuss the relationships that educators and students develop with industry and how they initiate those relationships. Then, you'll learn about the guidelines—based on current industry standards—that design organizations created to help educators structure their design programs. We'll highlight how those guidelines connect to design curricula and experiential education. You'll also learn directly from professionals working in the field who describe how client-based experiences help students develop empowerment on the path to gaining employment.

HOW?
WHO?
WHAT?
WHY?

Models for industry and community engagement

Throughout this book, we will toggle back and forth between describing partnerships with industry (for-profit businesses) and community (non-profit and civic organizations). Most designers work with clients across a spectrum of organizational types. But there are some differences, especially when first developing and maintaining organizational relationships.

DESIGN AGENCIES

One way for programs to engage with industry is to build relationships with design agencies, studios, advertising firms, and similar businesses. These interactions can be singular events or ongoing programming. A few forms of engagements between schools and agencies include:

- Inviting guest speakers from agencies to speak with your classes in person or virtually (also a great way to stay connected with alumni!)
- Coordinating studio tours
- Bringing in outside reviewers for project or portfolio critiques
- Co-sponsoring design events (e.g., an agency could pay for a visiting designer or film screening, and the university could provide a facility for the event)
- Working together for community service events, such as design marathons for nonprofit organizations
- Building internship pipelines to agencies
- Establishing sponsored research programs

Ideally, these will be mutually beneficial relationships. Students can gain real-world insights and industry connections. Design programs and faculty can stay more relevant by keeping up with industry trends. Agencies benefit from visibility and can mentor possible future employees. More than that, **we've found that many professionals *love* working with students** because it allows them to give back and gain teaching experience.

SPONSORED RESEARCH

At some institutions, educators have created relationships with external partners that are more intensive, and that often last longer than a single semester or term. Sponsored research is usually well-funded and allows students to focus on one theme or idea and build comprehensive research knowledge about a particular client and context. With these longer-term projects, students can jump in at any time during the work. For example, at North Carolina State University, faculty members Meredith Davis and Helen Armstrong have developed well-defined and recurring relationships with corporations like IBM and SAS. These more robust, research-oriented projects often lead to students being hired as interns following their coursework.[1] More on this in *Chapter 11*.

MINI-ACTIVITY

Research local design agencies. If you find one you like, try emailing to see if you can take a studio tour, or ask if they might be willing to speak with your class.

CLUBS AND ORGANIZATIONS

Many design programs also connect students to industry by developing student chapters affiliated with professional design organizations.

AIGA/DESIGN CLUBS

AIGA student chapters connect to local AIGA chapter boards that continuously develop programming to link students to professional designers. Students attend professional events, take studio tours, and participate in portfolio reviews and mentorship programs. In addition to engaging with professionals, student groups develop activities for fellow designers in their programs. These could include sharing internship experiences, giving resume and cover letter feedback, and inviting guest speakers to campus. They often host activities just for fun, too! This could include holiday parties, watching design movies, going to design events, and open studio time where people design together, making Valentine's collages or letterpressing holiday cards for example.

INTERNATIONAL SOCIETY OF TYPOGRAPHIC DESIGNERS (ISTD)

The ISTD is a welcoming group of type designers seeking to engage students from the UK, Ireland, the Middle East, North America, South Africa, and Australasia in the profession. They offer resources and events for students, including a highly competitive annual typography competition. If students are awarded during the student assessment scheme, they gain a lifetime ISTD membership. Regardless, through participation in the competition, students receive thorough feedback from educators and industry professionals on their design solutions. See *Activity 2.1* for an example ISTD exercise.

THE ONE CLUB

The mission of The One Club is to "support and celebrate the success of the global creative community," striving to support writers, art directors, designers, technologists, and artists. They also foster opportunities for emerging creatives to connect with established professionals—through events like portfolio night, workshops geared towards high school and college students, scholarship opportunities, and award competitions.

TYPE DIRECTORS CLUB

The Type Directors Club is a global community of graphic designers known for its prestigious competitions that help students gain exposure and feedback about their design work. Award-winning work is displayed in traveling exhibitions all around the world. They also sponsor events, post job listings, and offer scholarships.

STUDENT COMPETITIONS

Many design organizations also offer competitions, which can be a great way to get your work seen and acknowledged. It's also a way to stretch and grow your design portfolio when competitions have specific design briefs or challenges. Awards can also be positive resume boosters.

ALUMNI RELATIONSHIPS

Another great way to get connected to the design industry is through alumni. Many want to assist and mentor younger students and are happy to interact with you. In addition to design-specific organizations, you can participate in school-specific events for alumni. If you oversee social media for your program, consider developing an alumni group on one or more of the social media platforms.

NOT ALL EQUAL

While most design competitions are legitimate, some have hidden high fees you have to pay if you win. When in doubt, read the fine print or ask your professors for guidance.

ACTIVITY 2.1

Invisible Cities – ISTD example brief[2]

A new edition of Italo Calvino's novel, *Invisible Cities* is to be published. The publisher wants the book to form a radical retelling; its typography is to visually explore each of the cities, reflecting their characteristics and idiosyncrasies. The book is either to be a physical large format edition—at least 406mm × 254mm, which means you have the opportunity to think very carefully as to how the text will "own" the page—or an edition for digital natives that is to be designed for a smartphone, tablet, desktop, game console, or VR experience.

If you decide to create a book, you will have several decisions to make about its binding or layout—it can be traditionally glue bound, thread sewn, stab bound, it could be a concertina, a map, a dos-à-dos, or a format where the visual narratives interact and work with each other. There is no requirement to physically make your book, however, you will need to think quite clearly about how the book would be produced in an ideal world, and show that concept in some form or other (a Photoshop mock-up, or illustrator line-drawing, for example). You are required to produce the book as a PDF containing the cover, title page, and introduction, plus at least four tales interpreted typographically. A single page might contain one city—as the traditional print edition does—however, you may design it so that each double-page spread is one city, or several cites exist on one large opened-out page as a geographically placed map ... the choice is yours.

If you decide to create a digital/virtual experience, will the outcome be a dynamic one that works across several different platforms? Will it be a passive or interactive experience for the viewer? What are the conventions of a traditional reading experience that are now redundant? What do we take for granted that we no longer need?

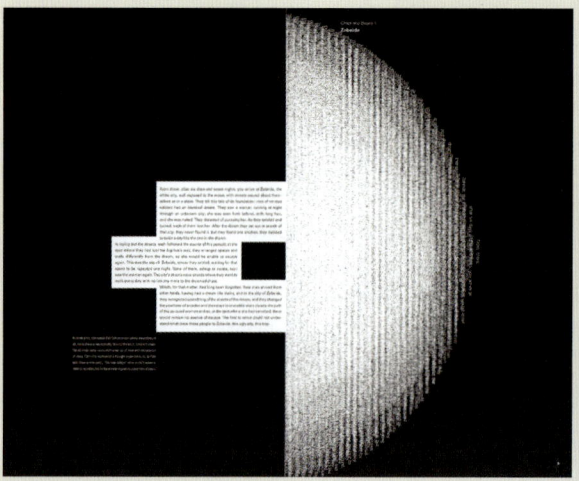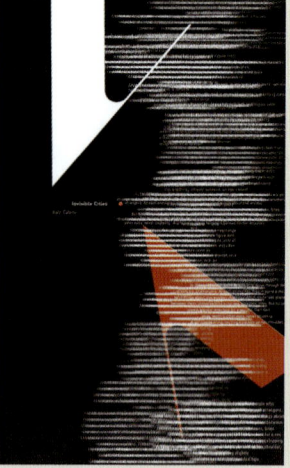

Source: *International Society of Typographic Designers* istd.org.uk (project by Barrie Tullett)

Student example: Beata Sarkadi | TU Dublin
Tutors: Brenda Dermody, Peter Maybury, Louise Reddy

Building relationships with community & civic organizations

In addition to working with industry clients and partners, many designers also choose to work with non-profit organizations and community partners. This work requires careful attention to ethics and participatory processes in order to achieve equitable outcomes. *Chapter 4* dives into much more detail about developing and maintaining these kinds of partnerships.

NETWORKING

Networking can be an effective strategy to connect with community organizations you are interested in working with. For example, when Penina Laker first moved to St. Louis, Missouri, to work for Washington University, she received training through the local regional arts commission. For seven months, she worked alongside artists, designers, musicians, poets, and spoken-word artists in one of the under-resourced neighborhoods in St. Louis. Together they explored how they could use their creative skills in arts and design as a tool for positive social change. Penina brought these connections and her local knowledge back to the classroom and built trusted, ongoing relationships with students and community partners in the city.

COMMUNITY OUTREACH OFFICES

Universities often have offices dedicated to developing relationships with their surrounding communities. Search for terms like community, outreach, engagement, and/or partnerships on your institution's website. If you find something, reach out to that office to see if they can connect you to people who might be looking for design services. And if they're not sure, tell them what you can offer! Providing a synopsis of the kinds of services you can provide can help them start to make connections in your community on your behalf.

CIVIC PARTNERSHIPS

Taking community outreach a step further, some institutions have developed more substantial ongoing civic partnerships with other organizations in their surrounding communities. Many of these initiatives focus on health, education, transportation, food, and business development. Connecting to these established interactions could be a good opportunity for you to leverage design's capabilities to facilitate creative communication and innovation.

MINI-ACTIVITY

What do you most care about? Brainstorm a list of organizations and causes that are meaningful to you. Later, you can use this list as a springboard for finding community partners, or as a starting point for a passion project.

MIND-MAPPING

Students from Washington University in St. Louis work on a collective mind-mapping activity to synthesize findings from research on assigned topics.

INTERVIEW: *Penina Laker, Design in social systems*

Penina Laker is a designer and educator whose work and research are centered around topics that utilize human-centered approaches to solving social problems.

The "Creative Practice for Social Change" minor is a recent initiative of the Sam Fox School of Design & Visual Arts at Washington University in St. Louis, to provide students with a deeper understanding of how to use creative practices in art, design, and architecture to address systemic economic, environmental, and social challenges.

How do you incorporate client work and community partnerships in your design classroom?
A classroom can be a laboratory for learning and creative problem-solving. In St. Louis, we talk about being aware of this notion of over-engagement and over-surveying, especially in those under-resourced communities and populations within a one-mile radius of our university. Students get that opportunity in a more controlled and protected environment to engage the community, while also being given the space to fail and not have as much pressure to know the answers.

What are some of the typical learning outcomes or goals for your students and these client and community-based experiences?
I want students to get an appreciation for the complexity that comes with trying to understand systemic socioeconomic and environmental issues and how these issues go into shaping the lived experiences of individuals—and also how they're shaped by policies in the different communities that they serve. I've found that this tends to come down to a systems-thinking approach. I think about supporting ongoing work versus how we can go on to address and develop solutions that solve problems. *Support versus solving* has become a learning opportunity for our students. They're constantly asking, "How can I, during this partnership, learn what our community partner needs so that we can best support and amplify those ongoing efforts?" What's great about this is that the students start to see themselves as this small additional part of that larger whole, not the "expert" taking over and doing all this work.

What strategies do you have to involve students in that initial collaboration and how do you help them learn how to do that?
Prior to students working in groups or being part of a small group that will work with a specific organization, I spend time asking them to reflect weekly on various topics they are interested in after being introduced to the different potential partners and the issues that we'll be looking at. What's great about these kinds of classes and community partnerships is at the end of the day, this is not a fictitious assignment or project. We are dealing with real-life scenarios. What happens is a group dynamic might impact outcomes that will go on to potentially impact the lives of people that we're working with, or at least what we've promised we're going to deliver. So a certain level of professionalism is expected with such projects.

How do you consider equitable practices when engaging students with external partners?
That's extremely important, especially given the audiences that our partners are serving. These are populations that are already under-resourced, underserved, and marginalized. We're constantly asking ourselves, "How do we think about the outcomes being inclusive?" I also recognize that because of the complexity of the topics and the kinds of issues our partners are wrestling with, I don't have all the answers to all the questions students might have. Before we engage in the projects, I introduce students to a range of practitioners and processes to help us design with and think about how to work with an equity mindset.

How do you evaluate students and their work with these community partnerships?
Each student group will develop a set of objectives or goals for their partner project after having spent time really engaging the partner and understanding where the opportunities are before they jump into designing. We work through identifying the goals of this project. What do you hope to achieve at the end of this project? And we work with the partner to say, Are these goals feasible? Did this sort of make sense? Are we missing the mark? And if we all say yes and sign off, then I come back to that and say, okay, what goals did we meet? And sometimes, the goals have not been met, and if something like that happens, students won't be penalized for missing that, as long as they paid attention to outcomes and process.

What are the biggest challenges of this kind of experience?
It takes time. It takes a lot more than our other traditional design-based classes. I've found that in teaching classes like this, the bulk of the work, if done well, comes from establishing those relationships with our community partners—it's genuinely building that trust. In the last five years, we have started to do a better job of talking about what compensating our partners looks like. Our Office of Engaged Practice has started to put together small grants to donate to just support our partners and the work that they do. Because our university has asked a lot of our communities and has taken so much, it's only fair that we consider equitable practices and that we also honor what they're bringing into the classroom.

What are the biggest rewards of this type of work?
There are so many rewards. We are Washington University in St. Louis, and we're always talking about how our positioning in the city is so critical. What does it mean for us to be *in, with, for* the city. It's part of this identity that our university is continuously trying to do better. And I think that classes like this provide that great opportunity for us to not only check the narrative, but hopefully establish something unique and different in the way that the community sees us and views us.

What advice would you give to a student who is about to begin a community partnership?
Have an open mind. Be ready to let go of any notions you might have of what community partnerships look like. Because if it doesn't turn out to be what you expected it to be, it doesn't mean that partnerships are unsuccessful. Community partnerships are unpredictable, but they can be so rewarding for students. So have an open mind and be ready to be challenged and to have your biases checked during this process. I would tell them to just really embody that mindset.

What advice would you give to faculty who are thinking about doing this kind of work for projects?
For faculty, just *know your why*. I know that may sound cliché, but just really spend some time thinking about the end game for you as well. Why do you want to engage in such partnerships in the classroom? For me, I knew I really wanted to learn about the place where I live and find ways to support ongoing efforts. And I knew that the classroom would be a good place for that. And so that has kept this going for me for over six years. ∎

Advice from educators

Putting this all together, how do we meaningfully connect learning goals and outcomes to our connections with industry and community partners? At the end of the day, this is about personal and professional development. *Chapter 3* examines this in detail, suggesting ways to think about how you can develop a sense of empowerment along this career journey. With the personal in mind, we asked design educators what advice they would give students as they explore opportunities in experiential education. Here's what they had to say:

> Collaboration is fundamental to all of this. We trusted the students, they trusted us and hopefully they trusted one another. But if there are ways to engage people in knowing that this is for the good of something beyond yourself, I think that that really helps.
>
> —Ryan Slone

> Have an open mind. Be ready to let go of any notions you might have of what community partnerships look like. Because if it doesn't turn out to be what you expected it to be, it doesn't mean that partnerships are unsuccessful. Community partnerships are unpredictable, but they can be so rewarding for students. So have an open mind and be ready to be challenged and to have your biases checked during this process. Embody that mindset.
>
> —Penina Laker

> Be open. The most important thing, I think, is to be open and to be curious and to trust the process and to trust the people you are working with. Being open also means communicating any discomfort you might have, or questions you might have, or challenges or problems you might see. It's about working together. We see this so much in practice as designers wanting to work cooperatively. This is a collaborative field.
>
> —Maria Rogal

> I always tell students to respect each client, whether big or small in terms of project, to humanize everything and have patience, not to skip a step in the design process. If you go one step at a time, even though it takes longer, you are much more aware of your own process and thinking.
>
> I tell students to stay grounded, know who they are and just breathe, because I think we forget to breathe. We just keep going as though it's some kind of a rat race trying to meet every deadline, every client expectation. Yes, we are a service industry and that is expected of us, to meet all of the deadlines. But then it's very easy to not take care of ourselves and our own mental health. So I'm like, breathe, go for a walk. Just observe.
>
> —Archana Shekara

Establishing standards and outcomes

Once you've developed relationships and possibilities for design projects, you need to be sure that you will achieve the learning outcomes of your program. Throughout this section, we will discuss best practices for design programs based on current industry standards, National Association of Schools of Art and Design (NASAD) guidelines, and the AIGA Design Futures. In addition to looking at how student-run studios fit within the context of design education, we will also dive into how the programs fit into the larger university context of community engagement and outreach. We explore capstone-level practicum courses, course-level outcomes, and provide advice and examples for assessment.

Most institutions use guidelines from industry and government organizations (such as AIGA and Design Council UK) as well as accreditation organizations (such as the Commission for Academic Accreditation and the National Association of Schools of Art and Design) to develop design curricula and ensure that students graduate with the skills and knowledge they need in order to succeed in the design profession.

AIGA has worked with designers to reflect on the skills and mindsets that new designers will need to have when they begin their careers.

Design encompasses a broad range of activities, so designers need to learn many different skills. AIGA's recommendations call for a multidisciplinary design education that moves beyond simple design investigations to situate projects within multiple contexts.

AIGA calls for design educators to examine the principles of their curricula and to determine whether they are preparing students for positions in emergent practices and "wicked problems" within a knowledge economy.[3] Along these lines, many client-based projects we're describing encompass more than just designing a logo. These projects are about understanding the needs or wants of a client or partner within a larger context, like the community or the marketplace. People now hire designers to use "design thinking" to tackle more complex problems and understand how smaller components of a design project fit into larger systems. This approach requires research, analysis, synthesis, and design skills like visualization, communication, and prototyping. It requires integrating more than one type of thinking— because you're often working with people from different fields with expertise other than design—into a multidisciplinary approach. Instead of just designing a poster or an object, you're thinking about everything that fits into a larger system.

MINI-ACTIVITY

Take a current or former project and examine the context in which it would or does exist. How does the context (location, audience, year, etc.) shape the perception of the design?

CHAPTER 2: *Connecting to industry & community*   37

COMMUNITY CONNECTION

Students at Washington University in St. Louis collaborated with the Center for Community Health Partnership and Research to develop a new system of materials.

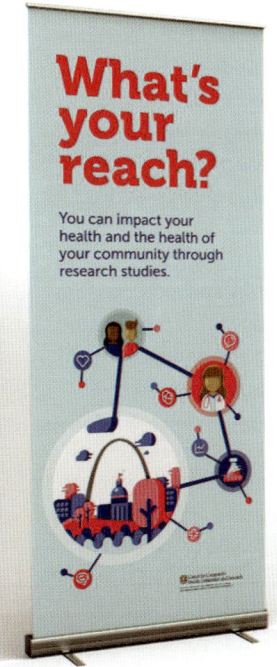

CHAPTER 2: *Connecting to industry & community*

DESIGN FUTURES

AIGA's Design Futures Trends

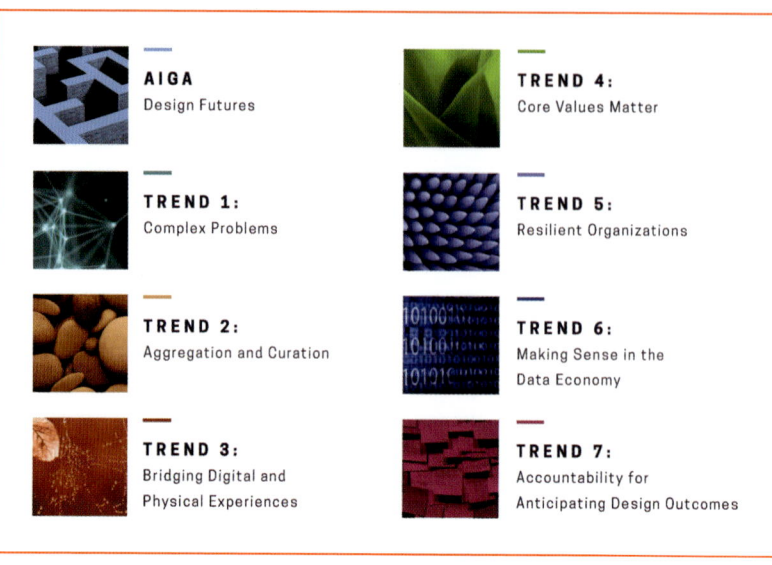

AIGA — Design Futures

TREND 1: Complex Problems

TREND 2: Aggregation and Curation

TREND 3: Bridging Digital and Physical Experiences

TREND 4: Core Values Matter

TREND 5: Resilient Organizations

TREND 6: Making Sense in the Data Economy

TREND 7: Accountability for Anticipating Design Outcomes

AIGA's college student competencies related to complex problems:
- Frame challenges across multiple levels, understanding the product/service within a system and a community.
- Identify relationships between products and services, people, places, and activities within a system/community.
- Leverage points within systems and communities where clients and partners create change and have impact
- Evaluate design solutions for more than aesthetic qualities (such as for their short-term impacts and long-term effects).
- Explore how different ways of thinking across disciplines can contribute to solving complex design challenges.
- Engage in collaboration, conversation, and decision-making that supports thinking across these multiple levels of a system or community.

In addition to learning skills like typography and programming, designers need to understand business skills. Experiential education opportunities offer a range of other skills that have to do with the holistic functions of a business.

Client-based projects can help you understand how companies operate and adapt and deal with various stakeholders and collaboration. With these skills, designers help make organizations more resilient and adaptable to change.

AIGA's college student competencies related to resilient organizations:
- Understand the role of design in the context of the overall activities of a business or organization (client).
- Conduct relevant research to develop a range of products, services, messages, and experiences.
- Analyze marketing and strategic plans to understand an organization's values, offerings, goals, and position in the marketplace or community.
- Construct a project management plan that identifies workflow, tasks, milestones, deliverables, time, assigned roles, and resources.
- Collaborate in teams to develop leadership, communication, critique, facilitation, and negotiation skills
- Understand the roles of technology in the operations of a business or organization.

Course and program outcomes

Design programs are accredited by different organizations depending on the country. In the United States, NASAD accredits many programs. Around the world, there are many other accrediting bodies, such as the Commission for Academic Accreditation (CAA) in the United Arab Emirates. NASAD (and other accrediting bodies) write guidelines to help educators develop in-depth, rigorous programs to prepare students for entering professional practice after they graduate. In addition to the aesthetic skills you learn in a design program, NASAD wants to be sure you also have experience beyond the formal exercises done in the classroom that orient you to the working profession.[4]

Students can accomplish this through internships, engagement with professional groups like AIGA, and of course, through experiential education projects with clients and community partners.

NASAD's criteria for communication design programs include many of the same outcomes that AIGA describes, including thinking at systems level, and understanding how design projects operate at multiple scales across different social, technological, and economic contexts. In addition, designers focus on integrating design processes with the activities of professional design practice.

EXAMPLE: UNIVERSITY OF FLORIDA (MINT DESIGN STUDIO)[5]

Design Program Learning Outcomes

Content
- Design visual form in response to communication problems.
- Exhibit principles of visual organization/composition, information hierarchy, symbolic representation, typography, aesthetics, and the construction of meaningful images.
- Exhibit appropriate use of tools and technology, including their roles in the creation, reproduction, and distribution of visual messages.

Critical thinking
- Exhibit the ability to describe and respond to the audiences and contexts in which communication solutions must address, including recognition of the physical, cognitive, cultural, and social human factors that shape design decisions.

Communication
- Produce solutions to communication problems, including the skills of problem identification, research and information gathering, analysis, generation of alternative solutions, prototyping, and evaluation of outcomes.

EXAMPLE: UNIVERSITY OF TEXAS (WKRM)[6]

Design program learning outcomes

wkrm allows students to acquire real-world design experience for academic credit, unlike anything that can result from a traditional classroom experience. wkrm provides students with real client-based experiences in a professional creative environment and strengthens relationships with local clients and communities.

By the end of the course, students should be able to effectively:
- Utilize the design process and strategies to initiate, develop, and execute design work.
- Critically analyze their own work and the work of others.
- Use a variety of research and design methods.
- Explain their design concept visually, verbally, and orally to a general audience.
- Contextualize and situate their design in a meaningful way for others to understand.
- Complete and present their work to the highest caliber.
- Demonstrate an understanding of standards and conventions of professional practice in design.
- Demonstrate the ability to work in a professional manner.
- Work collaboratively with designers, clients, and/or other stakeholders.

Client-based projects are where designers learn to integrate all of these attributes within an individual project. They research people, their activities, and their environments; they analyze those findings and develop insights; they use those insights to frame problems and generate ideas; and they create solutions that reflect the unique needs of their clients and partners. All of this requires skilled collaboration when working in interdisciplinary teams.

INTERNSHIPS

For those institutions that offer student-run studios, students might be able to substitute their semester- or year-long involvement in exchange for fulfillment of their internship credit.

Conclusion

We began this chapter by outlining some of the many ways design programs can connect to potential partners in both industry and communities. As those relationships are developed, educators work to ensure that the projects and courses achieve the program's learning outcomes. Industry organizations and accrediting bodies also inform those outcomes and goals. It's a lot to take in and manage, but when the pieces are well crafted and fit together, it really works to help you develop the collaborative and creative skills to succeed in professional practice.

Chapter 2 key concepts

learning outcome: an intended goal of a course, class, or workshop; framed in terms of what the student will be able to do at the end of the study

sponsored research: research (or creative projects) funded by an external company or organization

systemic issue: a recurring challenge that affects an entire entity (e.g., an organization or country), rather than just one individual

References

1. "Interview with Meredith Davis." Sept. 29, 2017.
2. ITSD. "Invisible Cities." istd.org.uk
3. AIGA. *Design Futures Research.* aiga.org/resources/design-futures-research
4. NASAD Handbook 2017-18. National Association of Schools of Art and Design.
5. University of Florida. catalog.ufl.edu/UGRD/colleges-schools/UGART.
6. University of Texas. catalog.utexas.edu/undergraduate/fine-arts/degrees-and-programs/#design.

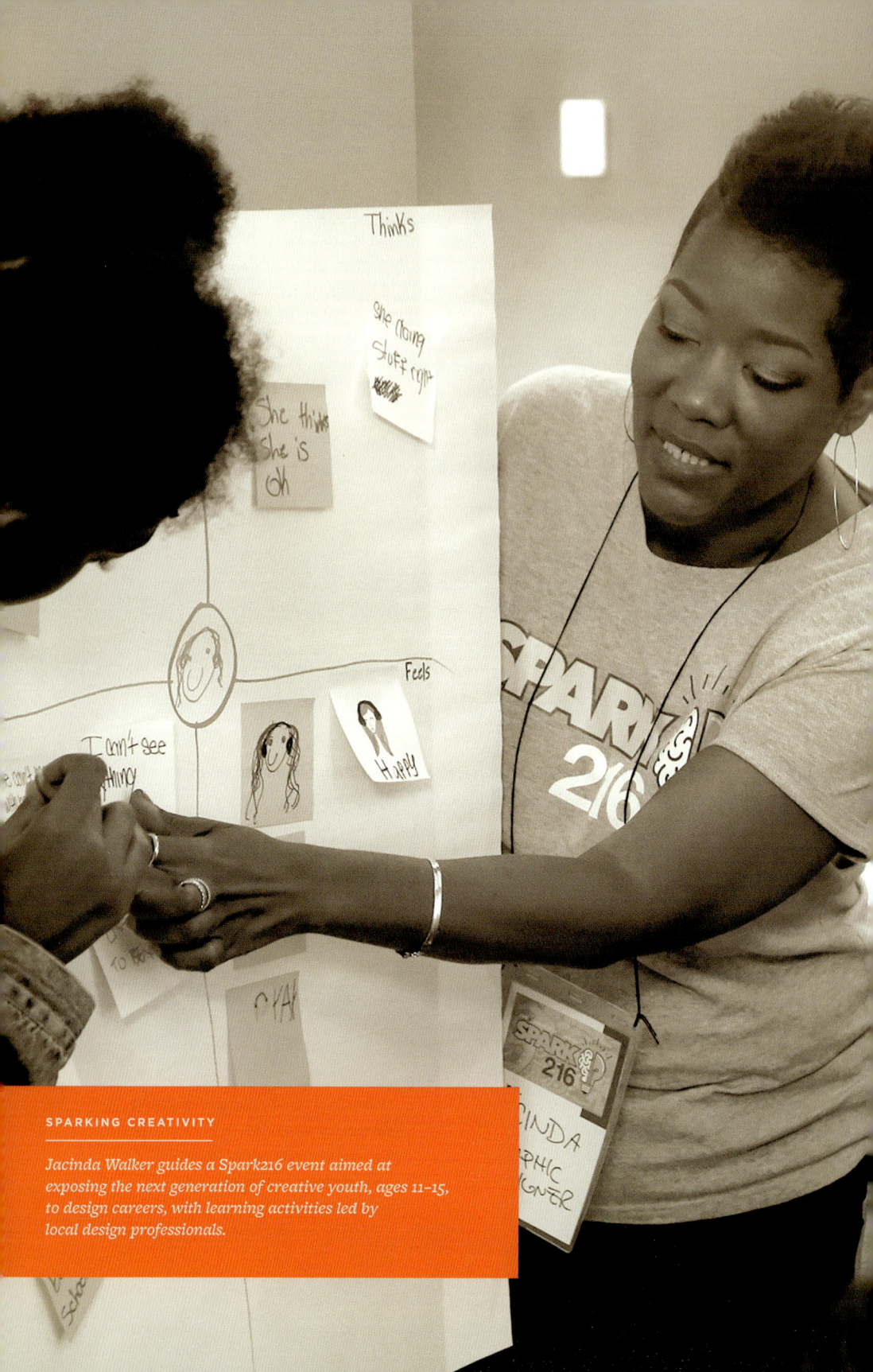

SPARKING CREATIVITY

Jacinda Walker guides a Spark216 event aimed at exposing the next generation of creative youth, ages 11–15, to design careers, with learning activities led by local design professionals.

Chapter 3

**CHAPTER WRITTEN BY
NAJLA MOUCHREK**

Becoming empowered

This last chapter of the Why? section takes a step back from design practice to focus on student growth as a whole person. We asked our friend and colleague, Najla Mouchrek, to talk about her research on empowerment, because we think this is the foundation of our goal as educators—to help you, our students, become the people you want to be. We passionately believe that experiential education through client-based projects can help you on your journey of empowerment.

Studio experiences can provide a sense of agency and purpose when taking on the responsibilities of guiding real-world clients and community interactions. By connecting reflection and critical consciousness to experiential education, you can identify a path towards success and develop the confidence and skills to thrive. You can examine equitable power sharing and successful collaborating by giving and receiving mentorship.

HOW?

WHO?

WHAT?

WHY?

Chapter 3 was written by Najla Mouchrek, Ph.D., who is an Associate Teaching Professor at Northeastern University in Boston, Massachusetts, USA. The chapter builds upon the *Integrated theory of empowerment in the transition to adulthood, developed in collaboration with Mark Benson,*[1] *applying it to experiential learning in design education and career development for design students. Najla is a designer and scholar interested in the potential of design-based methodologies to empower, create community, and promote transdisciplinary collaboration in processes of change towards sustainable futures.*

Empowerment in youth

For most traditional-age students, college is a time for navigating the complex transition to adulthood. Emerging adulthood—the life stage that runs roughly from 18 to 29 years old—is a time of opportunity to create positive self-identities and plans for future development, both professionally and personally. This transition is marked by a shift from relying on external authority, to taking ownership and responsibility for one's own life[2]—which makes exposure to diverse experiences and support for developing meaning-making and internal decision-making vital. Promoting empowerment in educational settings provides significant benefits for students, including healthy identity experimentation, gains in confidence, critical awareness, self-efficacy, and self-esteem.[3]

Empowerment grows from multiple sources—building from both changes in society and at a personal level. Individuals and groups empower themselves by actively working to gain greater control over their lives.[4]

It is essential to have welcoming, safe environments with opportunities for meaningful participation and balanced sharing of power[5]—spaces for engaging, reflecting, and affecting change together, empowering yourself and contributing to empowering your community.

When you are making the transition to adult life, **empowerment happens as an interplay between two foundational dimensions: self-direction, and developing a meaningful role in society.** This is the core of the integrated empowerment model (developed by Najla Mouchrek and Mark Benson).[6] See the model in *Figure 3.1*.

While the first dimension (self-direction) happens through internal processes of development, the second one (meaningful role in society) unfolds through external lived experiences that give you opportunities to actualize them. Each of these dimensions of empowerment emerges from four key catalysts—agency, sense of purpose, mentoring experiences, and engagement in community.

FIGURE 3.1

Model of the integrated empowerment theory: transition to adulthood, adapted from Mouchrek and Benson (2023).

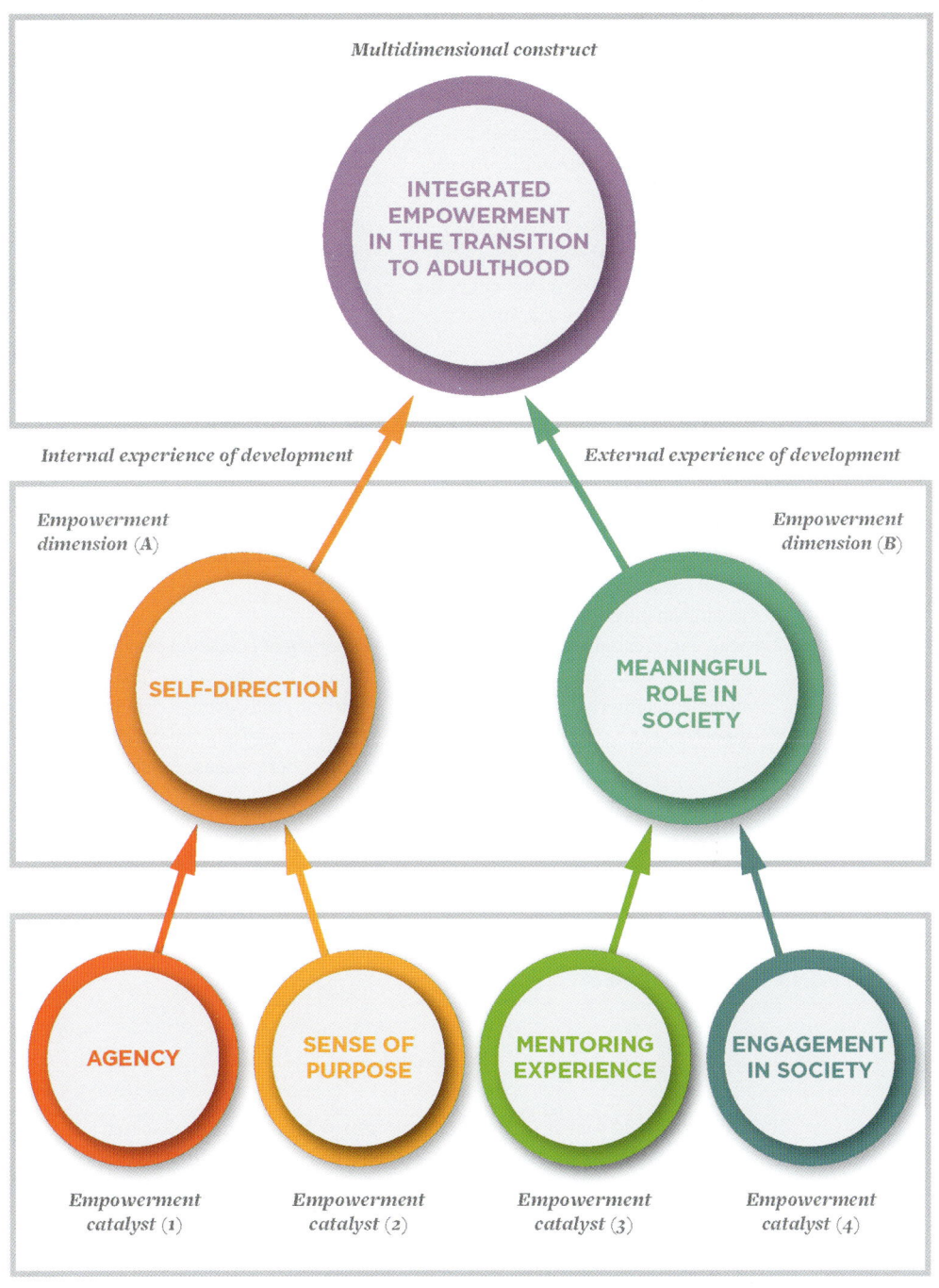

Model of the integrated empowerment theory: transition to adulthood

Catalysts of empowerment

Experiential education—such as the client-based projects described in this book—provides opportunities for you to develop the competencies, attitudes, and maturity needed to successfully transition to adulthood. More specifically, it encourages development of the fundamental catalysts of empowerment.

DEVELOPING AGENCY AND SENSE OF PURPOSE

Experiential education encourages the development of identity and agency. Experimentation with and reflection on lived experiences are essential for constructing your self and developing critical consciousness. Additionally, by focusing on purpose-driven experiences, experiential learning fosters a sense of meaning and purpose, another fundamental internal process for youth empowerment.

Experimentation. The process of construction-of-self occurs through experimentation: in adolescence and emerging adulthood, there is a richness of experience. In this period, the brain presents remarkable plasticity and is extremely sensitive to experiences.[7]

Experiential learning focuses on direct experience and in-context action and reflection (as discussed in *Chapter 2*). That is why it may address your need for diverse lived experiences in which you can make sense of what you learn by relating it to your personal way of understanding the world and directing your life.

Experiential education provides opportunities for exploration, flexible commitment, and deliberate choice-making. These actions help you develop agency and a coherent sense of identity that

---

INTERNAL DEVELOPMENT

What is agency?

It is your ability to understand yourself and what matters to you, be confident, and feel that you can control your actions. You are able to reflect critically about the world around you and have increasing autonomy to make your own decisions.

What is sense of purpose?

It is related to how much you search for meaning and purpose in life and to what degree your actions are oriented toward a greater good.

Together, agency and sense of purpose form self-direction:
the capacity to make thoughtful, self-authored, and strategic choices in life.

will guide your life path and facilitate your transition to full adulthood. Experiential education fosters the skills you need in order to become your own agent of change.[8]

Reflection. The reflective process that is part of experiential learning broadens perspectives, which is central to cognitive development in emerging adulthood. In this phase, you are developing advanced cognitive processes, including practical, flexible, and dialectical thinking abilities, greater processing of emotions, perspective-taking, and capacity for self-reflection.[9] In experiential education, learners are purposefully engaged in direct experience and focused reflection.

Reflection in context fosters the development of complex meaning-making processes, providing new and improved options for interpreting experiences and navigating environments.[10]

Purpose-driven learning. Purpose plays a powerful role in youth development.[11] A sense of purpose assigns meaning to your experiences, moving you toward fulfillment of your potential. A purpose-driven approach to experiential learning allows the development of real-life projects, connected to your aspirations, to contribute to (and be actively engaged in) societal change and evolution processes.

EXTERNAL EXPERIENCES

What makes mentoring experiences empowering?

Positive experiences with mentors are ones that provide guidance, support, and appreciation. In these partnerships, there is a balance of power and healthy collaboration.

What makes engagement in community empowering?

Engaging is beneficial when you feel you belong and have a place in the community. You are motivated to act, and your participation is meaningful and valued. You have space and support to use your talents and collaborate for the community's success.

Combined, mentoring experiences and engagement in community offer context, resources, and opportunities for you to gradually develop a meaningful role in society which will be key for your future as a citizen and as a professional.

ENVIRONMENTS FOR MENTORING AND COMMUNITY

By focusing on learning built from concrete realities and lived experiences, these learning activities have the potential to foster your empowerment through the development of healthy partnerships and opportunities for meaningful participation in local and global communities.

Mentoring and apprenticeship. Partnerships between professionals and students are central features for developing empowerment. Mentoring and apprenticeship are critical components of experiential education and provide a promising environment for multi-generational shared leadership and decision-making. Dialogue, balance of power, and collaboration are key components of these programs.[12]

Meaningful participation in community. Engaging in community issues promotes internal development as well as external community development.[13] Experiential learning may offer opportunities for building awareness of multicultural realities and diversity, and for working alongside community partners at local and global scales. Developing the capacity to contribute to our communities is one of the main goals of experiential education.[14]

FOR STUDENTS AND NEW PROFESSIONALS

For youth practitioners wanting to foster active real-world engagement, our empowerment model proposes an intervention strategy with four components:
1. establishing community
2. building agency
3. coordinating mentors, and
4. inspiring purpose (CAMP)

"In effectively establishing community, professionals, and volunteers foster a shared sense of belonging and provide meaningful opportunities for youth to effectively use their skills and potential. When communities encourage confidence-building and self-reflection, the context can bolster youth agency. Mentors who support and acknowledge the contributions of youth value their voice and preview paths to success. Interactions and shared constructions foster a sense of purpose, a desire to contribute to the greater good."[15]
— Mouchrek & Benson

CHAPTER 3: *Becoming empowered*   49

Three students are huddled around a computer screen, discussing sketches for a new logo commissioned by a local entrepreneur. Kai likes the sketch she developed, but she's not sure where to take it next. She says, "I got it to this point, but I don't know how to improve it. What do you all think?" Barry responds, "Well, remember how you created that poster design for our last client? You got stuck at a certain point there, too. But then you took a long walk, went to the museum, and got totally inspired. Which is really different from my thinking process. And it worked! So maybe try that again?" Kai is a little surprised—she hadn't noticed that was part of her process—and feels supported by Barry's feedback. "Wow, I guess you're right," she replies. "Thanks! I'll step away from this for now and see what inspires me outside the studio."

Janelle is a fourth-year student working on a project for a local nonprofit organization that focuses on food insecurity in the region. When she started college, Janelle didn't know much about how food insecurity impacts people. But now, as a lead designer in her college's student-run design studio, she's worked with this organization for two years and has become really passionate about its mission. The nonprofit's director, Shari, has become a mentor for Janelle, helping her feel confident in leading projects and contributing to the overall success of the organization.

FOR EDUCATORS

Higher education may play a significant role in youth development. Universities have great potential to be positive environments for students' growth and empowerment, hence the importance of designing the college experience while keeping in mind the perspective of youth development and needs. It is important to capture students' lived experiences during these years, and to understand what makes an empowering experience in formal and informal learning settings in college.[16]

What can you do to support youth empowerment in college settings?
- Provide a wide range of new experiences which require increasing complexity in reasoning and reflective skills.
- Foster awareness and reflection and encourage intrinsic motivation.
- Provide rich social contexts to encourage and inspire the expression of prosocial values (such as social justice, ecology, human rights, sustainability, diversity and inclusion, among others).
- Offer opportunities for engaging in meaningful roles and developing collective work that is authentic, interesting, fun and relevant to the real world.

EMPOWERING EXPERIENTIAL EDUCATION IN COLLEGE

When involved in experiential programs, students have increased feelings of empowerment and make positive changes in their lives and the community.[17] Experiential learning is considered an ideal approach to achieving the tenets of empowering education, because the results of direct experience are often concrete, easily identifiable, and applicable.[18] A consistent framework for experiential learning in college education provides opportunities for self-development, opportunities for working intentionally to promote empowering experiences, and offers transformative outcomes for students during the transition to adulthood.

In this stage of life, cognitive and social transitions lead to the development of personal values and the political principles that will guide you throughout adult life.[19] Autonomy, self-direction, and independence are at the core of emerging adulthood. **College should offer opportunities for you to practice the competencies needed to arrive at authentic, well thought out decisions and life choices.**

Also in this phase, the presence of peers activates your brain's reward system, and peer approval is closely linked to self-worth and validation of experiences and values. Therefore, it's important to have stimulating and rich environments for positive and healthy interaction within the community.

Empowering settings are those that:
- promote an empowering process (participatory, developmental) and an empowering outcome (enhanced control, capacity, and access to resources);
- promote a sense of community, encourage cooperation and collective decision-making;
- take into consideration your needs, interest, and abilities;
- frame the participation of youths as autonomous, responsible social actors;
- foster a critical understanding of the sociopolitical context. [20]

TRANSITION SCHOOL-WORK: DEVELOPING YOUR PROFESSIONAL IDENTITY

Being "career ready" means being able to develop and demonstrate a range of competencies that will prepare you for a successful transition from school to work. One of the essential competencies is the ability to identify and articulate one's skills, knowledge, experiences, and career goals.

Social changes in the past few decades have transformed the nature of employment.[21] The idea of a career as a fixed sequence of stages is not appropriate anymore. We now see increasingly individualized life and career courses. **Most people now change jobs more frequently** and tend to be in more short-term project-based work assignments. It requires flexibility to create one's own career opportunities, and to progress in a rapidly changing environment. Social contexts are increasingly calling for individuals to be able to reflect on their own skills and experiences, and to be context-aware, self-directed, active, and creative.[22]

Preparing for a future career requires agency and identity work besides reflection on your sense of purpose, priorities, and lifestyle decisions.[23] External experiences are also essential: exchanges with mentors, clients, and project partners and participation in teams, groups, and communities offer opportunities for you to apply and exercise self-direction, and to develop confidence and an understanding of who you can be as a professional in real-world contexts.

ACTIVITY 3.1

Create your career story

Today you are invited to craft your own story as you develop your professional trajectory.
- How do you think your experiences would align in a cohesive narrative of your own career?
- What are the interests and aspirations that guide you?
- What is the thread that connects your various learning and work experiences?
- Where do you think they are leading you?

Follow these guiding questions and start creating your career story.

A designer's professional identity

During your time in school, you start to gradually construct your professional identity as a designer. This identity is not separated from your personal identity and development—the two grow intertwined. In the words of Lawson and Dorst, being a designer becomes a part of your own self "because it involves so much that is personal, like your creativity, way of approaching the world's problems, your own history, learning style and view of the world."[24]

A designer's professional identity is complex and encompasses both developing a range of personal attributes and advancing several design skills. According to Kunrath and colleagues, the personal abilities are confidence, creativity, emotions, empathy, ethics, leadership, motivation, openness, responsibility, and social abilities. On the other hand, the design skills are cognitive abilities, cognitive strategies, personal communication, interpersonal communication, education-based knowledge, practice-based knowledge, managerial competency, and project management.[25]

This professional identity develops in the professional context as a product of the interplay of self-perception and social-perception.

In other words, to construct and advance your professional identity, you need help developing internally while having opportunities to apply your abilities and skills in the real world.

This is why experiential learning can be an excellent experience as you complete your training and form your identity as a designer.

Working as a designer in student-run projects with real-world clients can be an excellent opportunity to *learn through experience* how to:
- understand social, cultural, and professional contexts
- develop self-knowledge and find your strengths (agency)
- actively reflect on your motivations and values (purpose)
- engage respectfully and develop healthy, productive partnerships (mentoring)
- find a niche for yourself in the professional community (participation in community).

Reflection is an essential element in constructing your professional identity. It helps you understand the process of your transformation from "an expert student to a novice professional."[26] As you engage actively with learning processes and work experiences, reflection during and after these activities helps you develop two key components: knowledge for the profession and learning for professional work. Activity and reflection-in-action support your professional identity development in this phase. In *Activity 3.2*, we propose guiding questions based on the empowerment model.

ACTIVITY 3.2

Guiding your professional identity development

Think about your learning experiences in the classroom and outside the classroom. How do you see yourself developing the social abilities and design skills that constitute your professional identity as a designer?

AGENCY

To learn more about yourself and your abilities, think about your strengths when working in teams. What are your best contributions and characteristics when working on a team? To help you navigate these questions, we suggest you play the game Superpowers created by SYPartners.[27] The game leads you through interesting reflections that will help you define and intentionally craft your team participation.

SENSE OF PURPOSE

What are the goals and aspirations that inspire you? To think about what matters to you and how you would like to direct your professional life, consider questions such as, what global challenges would you like to contribute to solving? Look at the Sustainable Development Goals and targets (proposed by the United Nations)[28] and select the ones that you think are essential. Ask yourself, how can these global goals inspire my professional career? How can I align and direct my professional practice to help address one or more of these goals?

MENTORING AND COMMUNITY

How are your interactions with instructors, clients, mentors, and peers helping you to learn more about yourself and improving your practice? Would you like to look for mentors to support your growth?

How are these experiences allowing you to engage in meaningful roles and participate in different communities and organizations? What if you propose actively participating in a community you care about? What would it take?

How can these reflections support your work as a novice designer with real-world clients, community partners, and sponsored research projects? What must you learn to hone your skills and abilities to engage and offer your best contributions in these settings?

Superpowers card deck (SYPartners)

Sustainable Development Goals (United Nations)

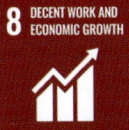

INTERVIEW: *Archana Shekara, Design Streak*

Design Streak is a capstone course for both the BFA and the BA/BS degree programs at Illinois State University. ISU students apply to the studio in their senior year after a portfolio review conducted by graphic design students. Approximately 8–9 students are involved at any given time. Design Streak was formed in 1981 by Pam Tannura. In the mid-2000s, Julie Johnson assumed leadership of the course, until 2016 when Archana Shekara took over as the faculty Creative Director. Archana's research is about cross-cultural awareness, cultural identity, and socio-cultural design.

What is the mission of Design Streak?

Design Streak strives to facilitate an interdisciplinary environment, promoting discovery, experimentation, and engaging in experiential and service learning. Design Streak studio combines design thinking and making, conducting ethnographic research, and collecting quantitative data to create new and authentic solutions to society's complex problems. The studio lab is committed to producing solutions of exceptional quality, and embracing design aesthetics to find a balance between form and function. Each project is valued for providing long-term sustainability with a strong emphasis on morality and social justice.

How do you initially make contact with your clients and non-profit organizations?

I've been living in Bloomington-Normal for 28 years and have served on several local, not-for-profit organization boards. This service helped me see gaps in the community. When I moved to Bloomington in 1994, it was a totally different place. I was very uncomfortable being Indian, walking around on the street, going to the grocery store, and wearing Indian clothing. So I would code-switch. I would be comfortable inside my own home, but when I stepped outside, I consciously behaved in a certain way to be accepted and understood. Undergoing several marginalized experiences empowered me to be the change and connect with diverse communities of people to build understanding, acceptance, and respect.

When I inherited Design Streak in 2016, I introduced new methodologies of design thinking and process, bringing my own expertise in service learning and socio-cultural design to create a research-based design lab. I wanted to foster a deeper engagement in experiential learning by partnering with community organizations that focused on social justice initiatives. I started creative directing and art direction so students could fully grasp the design process from initial client presentation to project execution. Word-of-mouth helped us grow from one client to 40 clients over six years.

In what ways are you providing mentorship, or how do you seek to empower students?

I believe mentorship is paramount. Students observe our giving. I'm a practicing Hindu, and I believe that teaching is the highest form of giving. Our students observe us while we mentor, and they learn from us. This includes how we behave and converse and how we empathize with and show respect to each other and the client. These are all critical learning skills, and I strive to bring a kind attitude and create a safe atmosphere in the studio so students are comfortable being themselves.

As a socio-cultural researcher, I understand that I need to unlearn and become more aware of my own biases. I come from a country with a different cultural mindset. But being in the United States for more than 30 years has given me the privilege of being myself—allowing oneself to be comfortable in one's own skin is imperative for students to witness. This is about mentorship as well. We are not just teaching students to create pretty pictures promoting client campaigns, we are actually helping them to become aware and sensitive, and to perceive design in a holistic way. Being a designer involves a holistic understanding of life. As mentors, it's central to know who we are as people, accept our vulnerabilities, and be authentic so we can then share that understanding with our students.

Since the studio model differs from a typical class, how do you evaluate your students?
I ask students to self-assess and reflect. Projects aren't graded. I want students to develop their own mindset, not work for a grade. Grades bring in ego and competition. I tell students, instead of using the word "I," especially when you're doing a group project, let's use the word "we." When we say "we," then it's more of a collective understanding, and it involves everybody, from clients to peers. I tell them, leave that ego outside the door. You are all here together, and we are all going to collaborate together. I also remove my ego as the faculty administrator.

What are the biggest rewards of this experience?
For students, the experiential learning prepares them for professional practice. It introduces them to diverse client expectations and the right kind of attitude they need to embrace. I tell students that cultivating humility will sustain us, and I share my stories of hardship as a woman and person of color, how people have treated me and my peers. For me, I have learned a lot from my students. I have learned to unlearn, be a good listener, and facilitate a safe space for students.

What are the biggest challenges?
Not every student has been introduced to concepts of racial equity, power and privilege, microaggressions, and implicit biases. Even though they might have taken classes, they haven't really thought about it. Practicing self-reflection with criticality is challenging, and it takes constant awareness to be mindful of their thoughts and actions.

What advice would you give to students?
Respect each client, whether big or small in terms of project, to humanize everything and have patience, not to skip a step in the design process so they can reach their goal faster. I tell students, while climbing a staircase, you take one step at a time, or you can skip steps to reach the summit. If you have skipped steps, you may reach the summit faster, but you're going to be tired. But if you go one step at a time, even though it takes longer, you are much more aware of your own process, endurance, and thinking.

Is there anything you'd like to share that I didn't ask about?
I believe history is repeating itself in terms of violence and xenophobia, and it's imperative that design education addresses these issues. Discussing race, racism, and classism is complex, but needs to be done since we live in a global and multicultural society. If graphic design education can address these kinds of perspectives, then we are doing something good. ■

Archana Shekara with student Hannah Piemonte
Photo credit: Lyndsie Schlick

Chapter 3 key concepts

agency: your ability to understand yourself and what matters to you, and your ability to be confident and feel that you can control your actions

empowerment: confidence in knowing that you have control over what happens to you and the choices you are able to make in your life

sense of purpose: this relates to how much you search for meaning and purpose in life and to what degree your actions are oriented toward a greater good

References

1. The empowerment theory and measurement instruments were published in Mouchrek, N., & Benson, M. (2023). "The theory of integrated empowerment in the transition to adulthood: Concepts and measures." *Frontiers in Sociology, 8*, 62.
2. Baxter Magolda, M. & Taylor, K. (2015). "Developing self-authorship in college to navigate emerging adulthood." In: Arnett, J. J. (Ed.). (2015). *The Oxford handbook of emerging adulthood.* Oxford University Press.
3. Chinman, M. J. & Linney, J. A. (1998) "Toward a model of adolescent empowerment: Theoretical and empirical evidence." *The Journal of Primary Prevention, 18*, 393–413.
4. Read more about empowerment: Cornell Empowerment Group. (1989). "Empowerment and family support." *Networking Bulletin, 1*(2), 1-23; Maton, K., Seidman, E., & Aber, M. (2011). Empowering settings and voices for social change: An introduction. In: *Empowering settings and voices for social change.* Oxford University Press; Rappaport, J. (1995). "Empowerment meets narrative: Listening to stories and creating settings." *American Journal of Community Psychology, 23*(5), 795.
5. Jennings, L. B., Parra-medina, D. M., Messias, D. K. H., Mcloughlin, K., & Williams, T. (2006). "Toward a critical social theory of youth empowerment." *Journal of Community Practice, 14*, 31–55.
6. Mouchrek & Benson, *op cit.*
7. Erikson, E. (1968). *Identity: Youth and crisis* (No. 7). WW Norton & Company; Steinberg, L. (2007). *Adolescence* (8th ed.). Boston: McGraw Hill Higher Education.
8. Schwartz, S. J., Côté, J. E., & Arnett, J. J. (2005). "Identity and agency in emerging adulthood: Two developmental routes in the individualization process." *Youth & Society, 37*(2), 201-229; Shellman, A. (2014). "Empowerment and experiential education: A state of knowledge paper." *Journal of Experiential Education, 37*(1), 18-30.
9. Berger, K. (2008). *The developing person through the lifespan.* 7th ed. New York: Worth Publishers; Arnett, J. J. (2014). *Emerging adulthood: The winding road from the late teens through the twenties.* OUP US.
10. Baxter Magolda & Taylor, *op cit.*
11. Damon, W., Menon, J., & Cotton Bronk, K. (2003). "The development of purpose during adolescence." *Applied Developmental Science, 7*(3), 119-128.

12. Desmond, B., & Jowitt, A. (2012). "Stepping into the unknown: Dialogical experiential learning." *Journal of Management Development, 31*(3), 221-230.
13. Browne, L., Garst, B., & Bialeschki, M. (2011). "Engaging youth in environmental sustainability: Impact of the Camp 2 Grow Program." *Journal Of Park And Recreation Administration, 29*(3).
14. Association for Experiential Education. (2013). "What is experiential education?" Retrieved from aee.org/what-is-ee.
15. Mouchrek & Benson, *op cit.*, p. 13.
16. Shellman, *op cit.*
17. Perrin, J. (2014). "Features of engaging and empowering experiential learning programs for college students." *Journal of University Teaching and Learning Practice, 11*(2), 2.
18. Santrock, J.W. (2014). *Adolescence* (16th ed.). McGraw-Hill Education.
19. Maton, K., Seidman, E., & Aber, M.(2011). "Empowering settings and voices for social vhange: An introduction." In: *Empowering settings and voices for social Change.* Oxford University Press; Lakin, R., & Mahoney, A. (2006). "Empowering youth to change their world: Identifying key components of a community service program to promote positive development." *Journal of School Psychology, 44*(6), 513-531; Frandsen, M. S., & Petersen, L. P. (2012). "From 'troublemakers' to problem solvers: designing with youths in a disadvantaged neighborhood." In: *Proceedings of the 12th Participatory Design Conference: Exploratory Papers, Workshop Descriptions, Industry Cases-Volume 2* (pp. 105-108). ACM; Chaskin, R. J. (2009). "Toward a theory of change in community-based practice with youth: A case-study exploration." *Children and Youth Services Review, 31*(10), 1127-1134; Zimmerman, M. A. (1995). "Psychological empowerment: Issues and illustrations." *American Journal of Community Psychology, 23*(5), 581.
20. Mouchrek, N. (2019). "Empowerment in the transition to adulthood: Supporting career exploration in college using participatory design (Doctoral dissertation, Virginia Tech)." Available at https://vtechworks.lib.vt.edu/handle/10919/90893.
21. Savickas, M. L., Nota, L., Rossier, J., Dauwalder, J. P., Duarte, M. E., Guichard, J., et al. (2009). "Life designing: a paradigm for career construction in the 21st century." *Journal of Vocational Behavior, 75,* 239–250.
22. Peavy, R. V. (1995). "Constructivist career counseling." ERIC Clearinghouse on Counseling and Student Services; Guichard, J., Pouyaud, J., De Calan, C., & Dumora, B. (2012). "Identity construction and career development interventions with emerging adults." *Journal of Vocational Behavior, 81*(1), 52-58.
23. Schwartz, Côté & Arnett, *op cit.*; Bernaud, J-L. (2014). "Career counseling and life meaning: A new perspective of life designing for research and applications." In: *The Construction of the identity in the 21st century: A Festschrift for Jean Guichard*, eds A. Di Fabio and J-L. Bernaud (New York, NY: Nova Science), 29–40.
24. Lawson, B., & Dorst, K. (2009). *Design expertise* (1st ed.). Routledge, p. 270.
25. Kunrath, K., Cash, P., & Kleinsmann, M. (2020). "Designers' professional identity: Personal attributes and design skills." *Journal of Engineering Design, 31*(6), 297-330.
26. Reid, A., Dahlgren, M. A., Dahlgren, L. O., & Petocz, P. (2011). *From expert student to novice professional* (Vol. 99). Springer Science & Business Media.
27. SYPartners (2017). What's your superpower? (Game/deck of cards).
28. United Nations Development Program (2017). Sustainable development goals.

Part two

What?

CHAPTER 4

Engaging with communities

CHAPTER 5

Finding focus & targeting clients

CHAPTER 6

Achieving learning goals

EXPLORING DESIGN

Jacinda Walker running a design workshop via her company, designExplorr.

Chapter 4

Engaging with communities

Client projects are an excellent way for students and institutions to engage locally, build partnerships nationally, and collaborate internationally. When you work with real people and organizations instead of hypothetical classroom scenarios, you can develop listening skills, learn to communicate across differences, and adjust to various collaboration styles. However, it's essential to approach this work ethically, and to consider how these partnerships are mutually beneficial rather than extractive. You can use responsible, reflective engagement strategies to foster reciprocal partnerships with lasting social impact.

This chapter will identify strategies to "design with, not for" communities, and will examine considerations of ethics and value.

HOW?

WHO?

WHAT?

WHY?

Design *with*, not *for*

Many of us are excited by the possibilities for design to have a real, meaningful impact on the world. We are drawn to projects that might improve people's lives. In the classroom, these projects come from community-based organizations that are mission-driven for social good. But when working on these projects, we want to be careful not to adopt a "savior" mindset, thinking we know what's best for others without seeking their input. With that in mind, designers increasingly approach their work with a mindset to "design with, not for" their clients.[1]

You shouldn't presume to know what is best for a person, client, or community. Designing *for* leads to unequal power relationships. Designing *with* leads to better, more sustainable design solutions that clients and communities will actually use and enjoy.

To design ethically and responsibly, you need to practice self-reflection before engaging with clients and community partners. After that, your design processes can help create an equitable interaction that starts to equalize power.

> *Design has been there, it's always been the fabric of our society. We make something out of nothing every single day ... And if we are able to do that, why are we not at the table when it comes to addressing systemic oppression? Why are we not at the table when it comes to social justice? Why are we only called when it comes to commercially-based projects but not things around social good? I wanted to flip that on its head and lead our own path with the activists.*

—Antionette Carroll, *Creative Reaction Lab*[2]

Knowing yourself

Before you even start designing, it's important to know and understand yourself. We all have different identities, backgrounds, experiences, and beliefs that we must be aware of when collaborating with others. John Dewey, an influential philosopher and educational reformer active in the early 20th century, believed that we learn more from reflecting on our experiences than we learn from just the experiences themselves.[3] If you don't know how your own identity and background shape who you are and how others perceive and respond to your words and actions, you won't be able to collaborate effectively.

Gaby Hernández, who managed Mint Design Studio at the University of Florida, and who now teaches at the University of Arkansas, has developed an approach for students to practice self-reflexivity. Gaby feels that client work in the classroom allows students to become vulnerable and open to exploring their own backgrounds in a safe environment. She asks students to **define their assumptions and biases and then reflect on those assumptions and challenges** at a few points during the semester. This also allows students to become aware of each other's differences and more conscious of how those differences can shape their interactions.

MINI-ACTIVITY

Consider how your biases might affect how you interact with others—your peers, instructors, and clients.

Understanding others

In addition to knowing ourselves, it's also critical that we work toward understanding others and their lived contexts. Gaby Hernández also assigns readings that introduce students to biases, privilege, nostalgia, sense of place, and issues related to immigration, acculturation, and colonialism. Students respond to these readings by thinking about how the concepts apply to their own lived experiences, and then they also hear the responses from their fellow students. Learning about differences in their experiences and perspectives helps them to check for their own biases, and to better understand privilege (or lack thereof). This exploration starts to build greater tolerance and empathy for others. Then, when this knowledge gets translated to design, students begin to see how design impacts people differently in everyday life, depending on accessibility, affordability, and transparency. A design solution that works for one person might not work for many others. Exploring the lived experiences and knowledge of others helps us become better designers.

Intersectionality

Understanding others also requires a more nuanced, complex approach to identity. Intersectionality is a framework that highlights the interconnectedness of different social identities, such as ability, class, gender, race, and sexuality, and how those identities interact to shape our experiences. It recognizes that individuals may encounter multiple forms of oppression and discrimination simultaneously and cannot be fully understood by only considering one aspect of identity.

In a design context, intersectionality can inform how we approach problem-solving and community engagement. It reminds us to consider the diversity of identities within any given community and to ensure that our solutions are inclusive and respond to the needs of all individuals. The diagram below offers a visual representation of how different identity markers can shape how we see the world and how the world sees us. **By centering intersectionality in your design work, you can create more equitable and sustainable solutions.**

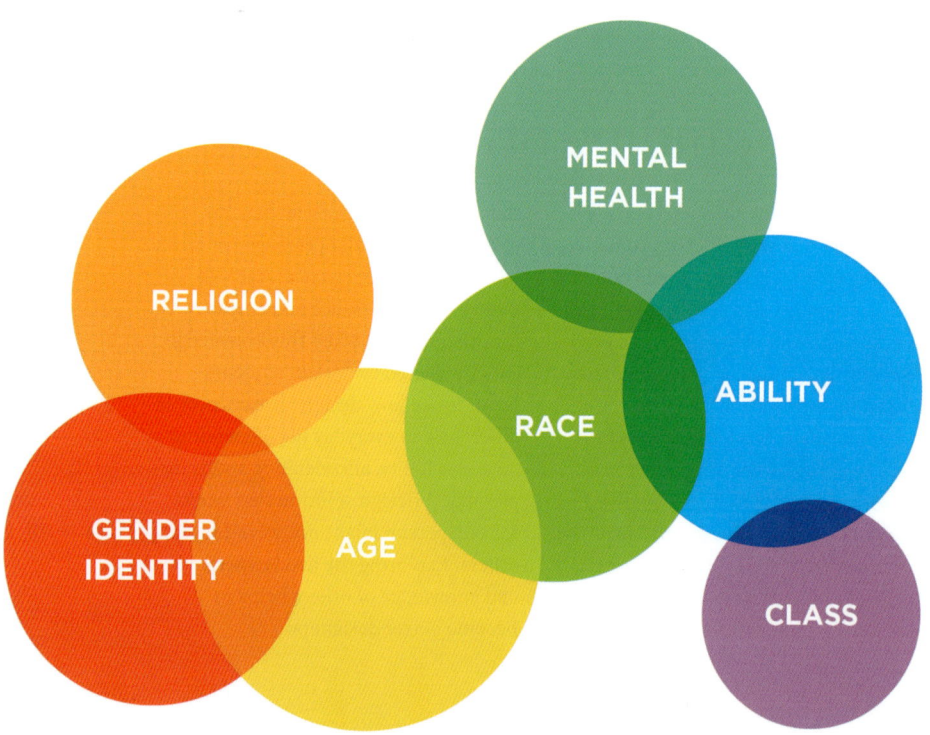

Intersectional social identities

Empathy

Many designers seek to cultivate empathy—the ability to feel what another person is feeling or to put yourself in the position of another person—in the initial stages of a design project. This human-centered design approach prioritizes a focus on what the users of a design actually want and need and do, not what any individual designer thinks they want, need, and do.

Design researchers Deana McDonagh and Joyce Thomas identify four areas for successfully designing with communities: shared language, collaboration, ethnography, and empathy.[4] They explain that "when training young designers to consider the wider community (people unlike themselves) during the design process, it has proven extremely valuable to take them outside their comfort zones, by seeking to develop empathy with the end user for whom they are designing." To collaborate and develop a shared working language, groups must work together to define and redefine terms to establish a common language and design processes. An ethnographic approach to design involves observing people in action, ideally resulting in seeing insights firsthand. **Empathic research methods should consider** *what people say, what they do, and how they feel.* Only through multiple modes of engagement can designers fully understand the communities they are designing with.

However, designers must be careful not to privilege their interpretations of how other people feel over people's own interpretations. Again, intersectionality can be a useful concept here to think about your power and privilege when interpreting someone else's lived experiences. **Empathy has limits because we can never truly know what someone is feeling.** It's better to try to share an experience with others than to transfer their experience to you.[5]

Eric Benson, a professor at the University of Illinois, encourages designers to "listen, not hear," stating that "it is important to put the community interests and needs above that of the designer. We all want to get something out of a creative project individually; however, when working with a community, listening to their desires is crucial and necessary."[6] Designers can dive even deeper by joining the community (when appropriate), because a fully invested community member understands the group's needs and wants. Working with a representative sample—not just one or two people—is critical to gaining such insight. One way to begin this process is to listen with empathy.

MINI-ACTIVITY

Find a partner. Dedicate one person as listener and the other as sharer. Set a timer for five minutes, during which the listener can only speak in questions. Then, switch roles and repeat.

Listening and communicating across difference

By synthesizing all these practices and concepts—self-reflection, understanding others, intersectionality, and empathy—we learn to listen and communicate across differences. This process requires designers to confront their biases and assumptions before engaging with clients or communities. In *Collaboration in Design Education,* Marty Maxwell Lane and Rebecca Tegtmeyer state that "both faculty and students inherently have a cultural bias that needs to be discovered and openly discussed in order for cross-cultural collaborations to be successful." [7] To successfully confront these biases, participants should strive to let down their defensiveness and be vulnerable.

Self-improvement, cultural awareness, and humility are processes that take time.

Students can begin in the classroom by sharing their experiences, but this is only possible when the classroom is a safe space where dialogue and discussion are valued and respectful. However, no one should feel forced to share. Additionally, participants should recognize that even in a diverse classroom, only a small sampling of people are represented, and the needs of clients and communities are likely to be very different from the needs of you and your classmates.

Equitable design processes

Now that we've established the need to understand ourselves, the people we're working with, and the contexts they live and work in, let's talk about the details of the design processes themselves. There are many ways that designers try to work with methods and practices that share power and lead to more equitable outcomes. We identify just a couple of approaches here, but there are many others.

CO-CREATION

Co-creation is a design approach in which designers intentionally seek to design with, not for, users and participants. In *Design is Storytelling,* Ellen Lupton states, "When developing a new product, service, or app, designers often seek knowledge from users. Co-creation activities range from evaluating existing solutions to generating new ideas. In co-creation, designers work with users in order to understand the context of a project and learn how new solutions could improve people's lives."[8] Lupton recommends using design activities such as focus groups and brainstorming sessions.

In *Convivial Toolbox: Generative Research for the Front End of Design*, Elizabeth Sanders and Pieter Jan Stappers write from the premise that everyone is creative and can contribute to the design process by using well-developed, hands-on methods and tools.[9] They define co-creation as a collective creative activity that more than one person does together. They categorize the co-creation process by how people interact with those methods: what people say and think, what people do and use, and what people know, feel, and dream. These methods and the kind of knowledge they generate are visualized in *Figure 4.1*.

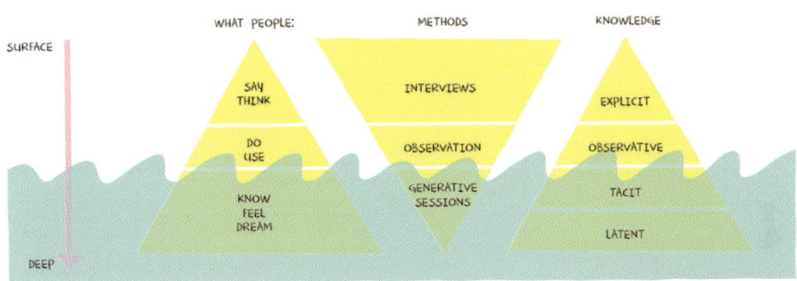

FIGURE 4.1

Methods that study what people say, do, and make can help us to access different levels of knowledge.

© Sanders & Stappers

PARTICIPATORY DESIGN

Participatory design is an approach developed by designers in Scandinavia in the 1970s. It was intended to equalize power in relationships between designers and the people they design with, and designers continue to use its methods to advocate for and with marginalized and oppressed communities. Because these methods often take longer and are less profit-oriented, they are often used in community-based contexts.

INCLUSIVE AND MULTISENSORY DESIGN

Sina Bahram encourages designers to think about an inclusive design approach that "recognizes that people have multiple forms of identity and difference, including age, ability, language fluency, socioeconomic status, cultural background, and so on. Accounting for those differences doesn't mean making everyone the same."[10] **One way of being more inclusive with your methodology is to design for multiple senses.** A multisensory design approach creates a richer experience while also accommodating those relying more heavily on one sense.

ACTIVITY 4.1

Brainstorming

Brainstorming is a group activity that seeks to generate many ideas and concepts about a specific challenge. Research shows that visualizing this activity helps to develop one's fluency in thinking.[11] *Basically, it's a combination of sense-making and mapping. A small group of people can generate lots of ideas together. Then, they organize those ideas and identify common themes.*

Best practices for brainstorming:
- Quantity over quality
- Defer judgment
- Practice active listening
- Encourage wild ideas
- Using open-ended prompts like, "How might we …?" and "What if …?"
- Build on the ideas of others
- Stay focused on the topic
- Have one conversation at a time
- Make thinking visible (drawings, diagrams, images, notes).

The intention is to generate as many ideas as possible and to build on each other's ideas. However, this can become a bit overwhelming (and is not always terribly productive) if we don't apply some structure to the process. Using a visualization framework (kind of like a graphic organizer) can help provide this structure:
- **Brainstorming webs (like a mind map)**: build off central big ideas and connect related ideas to those.
- **Tree diagrams:** helpful when you need to communicate hierarchies, describe categories or classifications of items, or relationships between ideas.
- **Flow diagrams:** suitable for a sequence of events, communicating a process, or showing cause and effect between related elements.

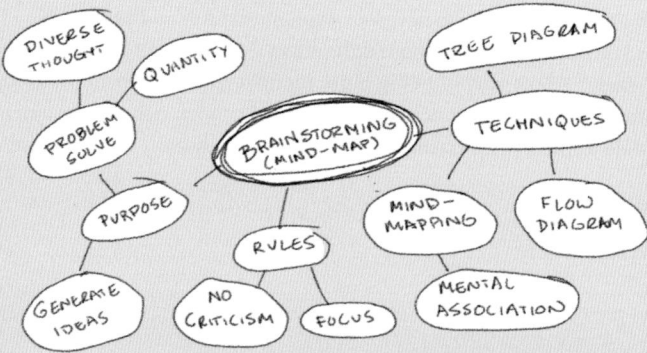

(Adapted from Martin and Hanington's *Universal Methods of Design*)

Bahram poses several questions to consider while designing. While they are specifically focused on exhibition design, they are worth reflecting on for all design scenarios:

1. **Equitable use:** design so that visitors get a similar or equitable experience even if they have different functional limitations.
2. **Flexibility in use:** create multiple ways for visitors to interact with the environment.
3. **Simple and intuitive use:** ensure that people with different knowledge or experiences can use the information being presented.
4. **Perceptive information:** develop ways for visitors to interact with the information or environment if they have a sensory disability.
5. **Tolerance for error:** allow visitors to easily return to a starting point (physical or digital).
6. **Low physical effort:** foster ways for visitors to appreciate the design without needing much physical effort or dexterity.
7. **Size and space for approach and use:** design ways for visitors to get close to and manipulate the environment or information, independent of posture or other physical limitations.

> **MINI-ACTIVITY**
>
> *Analyze your design. See if there's a way to incorporate additional senses and move beyond the visual.*

Some physical differences may be apparent, but many are invisible, such as how we each interpret our surroundings and our cognitive processing of information. Additionally, our memories impact our perceptions. Not everyone has tasted hot chocolate, smelled fresh lavender, broken a bone, or given birth. While some experiences are more common than others, remember not to design with the assumption that your audience has had the same life experiences that you have.

Co-creation, participatory design, and multisensory design are just a few of the many innovative ways designers try to make design processes more inclusive and equitable.

Identifying potential ethical issues

No matter which design processes and methods you use, ethical issues always exist. Some designers have created codes of ethics or principles to help guide them through projects and decide which projects to take on.

Adrian Shaughnessy writes that "all the necessary qualities to be a designer can be boiled down to three essential attributes that we need to combine with talent and craft skills: cultural awareness, communication skills, and integrity."[12] Your integrity—how honest you are and your moral principles—shapes you as both a person and a designer. Take a moment to reflect on what matters most to you.

Meaghan: One of my goals is to try to leave the world just a little better. This means treating people with kindness and respect and considering what I put into the world—from garbage to the artifacts that I design. I try to not leave too great of a carbon footprint, and remember that the words I use matter.

Jessica: I am continually developing and refining my own "critical reflexive praxis" where I use ideas that are important to me (like feminism and anti-racism) and try to put those into my design practice and interactions with others. Then, I constantly reflect on whether my words and actions embody those ideas.

On the following pages are a few examples of how designers infuse ethics to their projects and ideas for your reflection.

ACTIVITY 4.2

Write your own code of ethics

You can use one as a springboard or start from scratch. Get your group to write out ideas on a whiteboard, sticky notes (digital or analog), etc. You can do this as a team or start individually each writing out a few thoughts. Starting this way might be one way to "hear from" some of the quieter or more introverted among you.

Here are a few questions/considerations to get you started:
- What are some potential ethical issues?
- What do you do when a client asks you to do something you disagree with?
- What do you value?
- Sustainability (e.g., have you considered sustainable packaging and production?)
- Morality (e.g., would you develop advertising for a cigarette company?)
- Impact (e.g., what are the potential impacts of your design?)

INTERNATIONAL COUNCIL OF DESIGN

Professional code of conduct for designers

We contend that what is called "being a professional" is a combination of three elements. A professional has a commitment to:

- *a high standard of professional performance*
  Ensuring personal capacities to provide high-standard design services; this is based on initial and ongoing education, and a professional approach, mindset, and outlook.

- *a high standard of professional conduct*
  Integrity, honesty, transparency, etc.; this relates to ethical practices and relationships with clients, collaborators, and colleagues.

- *a high standard of professional responsibility to society*
  This relates to professional obligations to the greater community, humanity, and the planet.

Read the full code at
theicod.org/storage/app/media/resources/ICO_Professional_Code_of_Conduct.pdf

A DESIGNER'S CODE OF ETHICS BY MIKE MONTEIRO

A designer is first and foremost a human being.
A designer is responsible for the work they put into the world.
A designer values impact over form.
A designer owes the people who hire them not just their labor, but their counsel.
A designer welcomes criticism.
A designer strives to know their audience.
A designer does not believe in edge cases.
A designer is part of a professional community.
A designer welcomes a diverse and competitive field.
A designer takes time for self-reflection.

See the full Code of Ethics with additional description at
deardesignstudent.com/a-designers-code-of-ethics-f4a88aca9e95

NORTH CAROLINA STATE UNIVERSITY

Ethical design canvas inquiries
by Shadrick Addy & Victoria Gerson

PROJECT

- **System:** How and where will the system live within society/environment?
  What are the roles of the stakeholders within the system?
  How will the system be influenced/revised by participants?
- **Design brief:** How will the brief be executed, avoiding negative impact and responses from stakeholders?

DESIGNER

- **Morals:** How will working on the project influence my personal moral ethos?
- **Bias/prejudice:** How will my personal bias/prejudice inform my contribution to the project?

CLIENT

- **Values:** What are the values of the client's business?
  How does it align with my morals?
- **Services:** How are the values reflected in the services provided?

STAKEHOLDER

- **Target audience:** How can the system be informed by and uphold the target audience's ethos and values positively?
- **Edge cases:** Who am I leaving out?
  How can the design be more inclusive, acknowledging their potential participation within the system?

RESEARCH

- **Methodologies:** How does my research study and methodology inform my:
  understanding and interpretation of the design brief?
  understanding of the context of the system?
  understanding of how the stakeholders might respond?

PROCESS

- **Design (in):** How are the images reflecting the client and stakeholders' values?
  How is the visual language communicating a positive message to the stakeholders?
  How are the materials used contributing to the sustainability of the environment?

Review/considerations:
What are the potential cultural and social implications of this design project?
How does it uphold the values of I the designer, my client, and stakeholders?

Read more at:
academics.design.ncsu.edu/ands0/2019/05/20/reflective-tools-and-ethics-in-design

Collaborating at different scales

There are different approaches to engaging with community partners and developing reciprocal partnerships. Depending on the size and scope of your program, you can utilize one or more of these strategies.

CONNECTING WITH LOCAL ORGANIZATIONS AND AGENCIES

Most projects are at the local level, such as your own college or university, or other businesses and organizations within your geographic area. Design educators also develop collaborative partnerships with local design firms and agencies. Universities seek to build relationships with local communities to fulfill their mission of serving the public good. This effort intends to be a "collaboration between institutions of higher education and their larger communities for the mutually beneficial exchange of knowledge and resources in a context of partnership and reciprocity."[13] Experiential education, like student-driven client work, is part of this goal, as are other approaches like service learning, internships, and community-based research.

CREATING A SOCIAL ENTERPRISE

Some take it further and create a social enterprise to develop collaborations and client partnerships. Jacinda Walker created designExplorr, a social impact organization that seeks to "address the diversity gap within the design profession by expanding design education and raising awareness among community partners."[14] They work towards this goal by collaborating on educational youth programs, coordinating diversity-building initiatives, and connecting stakeholders to resources. As we write this, Jacinda and her team are building a 1,800 square foot Experiential Learning Center, a storefront space in downtown Cleveland, Ohio that will offer after-school programming, pre-college readiness courses, community tech teach-ins, and more.

NATIONAL COLLABORATIONS

Some design programs have developed national collaborations through a single project or a longer-term, sponsored research approach. For example, Helen Armstrong at North Carolina State University has facilitated student projects with large corporations. (Check out the case study in *Chapter 11* for more about Helen and her students' work.)

INTERNATIONAL COLLABORATIONS

Lastly, international collaborations are an exciting opportunity for students to work with clients, community partners, and fellow design students from other countries. In *Intercultural Collaboration by Design*, design educators Kelly M. Murdoch-Kitt and Denielle J. Emans write about how their students have collaborated across continents—Kelly in the United States and Denielle in Qatar.[15] When it works well, students develop shared goals and then use co-creation to innovate on design projects.

INTERVIEW: *Jacinda Walker, designExplorr*

Jacinda N. Walker, MFA, Hon. D.A., is renowned for her work in design, diversity, research, and strategy. She is the founder and creative director of designExplorr; a social enterprise whose mission addresses the diversity gap within the design profession.

designExplorr is a design education and social impact organization whose mission is to change the face of design.

What are some of the ways you work with K–12 students?

We have nine programs that come out of six different impact education modules. We create programs, workshops, activities, summer camps, after-school programs, and our main program, the Design Learning Challenge. There are Takeovers where we come to your classroom, and we totally take over. We also do Digital Design Workshops, which are our segue to technology. Unfortunately, many of our organizations don't have that tech piece.

In another program, we have a four-workshop bundle called "DesignIS." And so *DesignIS*: creative, *DesignIS*: change, *DesignIS*: cyber, *DesignIS*: careers. We've been doing these as introductory opportunities for organizations, schools, and educators to begin the conversation and introduce their youth to design.

How do you connect to those partners?

Two things. There are good partners and bad partners. Defining what your expectations are for your partner is critical. Be very clear about that. And after you get to that place, then you can pick good partners, right? Then you can recognize it. Being able to do those types of things helped me to really see the difference between good partners and bad partners. My friend always says, maybe it's allies. Maybe what you're seeking are allies, not partners. So, as I continue to grow designExplorr, I'm always looking for partners, but it's the allies that make it special.

Could you describe a favorite project you do or something that can really bring it to life for people?

We use a re-imagined design thinking process at designExplorr—written, developed, designed, and presented by me. I use this design thinking method because I was finding that the process that IDEO utilizes, it's beautiful. But it's hard. It might be hard for you to understand empathy. For people who are in survival mode, talking about empathy first was unsuccessful. And I was like, I'm going to redo this.

It was difficult to connect, and it's already hard enough to be something you haven't ever seen before. It is hard. But when I let them discover through a design activity and then we talk about it, then they're like, "What's that thing called when you put your name in and your mark your thing on it?" A logo. If you like doing that part, that's graphic design.

So I don't name "design" for them, I allow them, through our re-imagined process, to name it. It's all based on this level of giving them creative confidence with their thinking. So we have to empower their thinking.

What are the biggest challenges of these kinds of experiences?
I would be remiss if I didn't say finances aren't an issue, right? I also think one of the biggest challenges that I have is access. Like I just shared with you before, I don't work in a lot of privileged places. I don't work in a lot of rich communities. It's hard for me to find the partners, allies, and interested people who would be willing to pay and work with my students.

What are the biggest rewards?
I regularly get lots of young-people-love. My mentees go hard for me. They will show up.

What are your future plans?
We're opening a new space that I've been dreaming, working, and—visioning for many years—is our 1,800 square foot Experiential Learning Center. Ultimately, I want to have a pre-college residency program. The barrier is that many black and brown kids aren't going be able to afford this kind of experience. But through the experiential learning piece, we will be able to create workforce-based opportunities. ∎

Jacinda Walker in the fall of 2016 at the Las Vegas' Walter Bracken STEAM Academy. Developed with Playbuild: Professional designers worked alongside 87 fourth graders to address financial literacy. Students workshopped and used design thinking, to reach a variety of solutions, from "Moneyland" and redesigning cash flows, to addressing what transactions feel like to the impaired and rethinking financial service access.

Conclusion

As you can see, there's a lot to think about when engaging with communities on design projects. Otherwise, you run the risk of an extractive interaction with community members, one in which students and universities benefit, but partners are left without much to show for the exchange. The first step in any engagement is to try to know yourself and others through an intersectional lens that allows for empathic approaches and methods. Then, working with equitable design processes can help equalize power imbalances and generate solutions that become far more valuable and enduring because they are co-created with community partners. Layer in some ethical approaches at multiple scales—local, national, and international—and some successful, rewarding collaborations can start to happen.

DEVELOPING DESIGNS

Designer, Trevor Finney, guides Virginia Tech students through a critique during the design marathon, DesignUP.

REFINING SYSTEMS

Faculty, Patrick Finley, gives feedback to students developing a brand identity for a local nonprofit.

LEARNING FROM INDUSTRY

Students from Washington University in St. Louis consulting with a local environmental graphic designer and fabricator.

INTERVIEW: Patrick Finley, DesignUP

Are the students compensated, or are they provided anything in exchange for their work?
They're not compensated. But a few things came out of DesignUP that I wasn't initially anticipating. First, two of our students were actually hired by their design mentors for internship roles. The event was essentially like an interview. It's almost the best interview possible because you're working with this person for seven hours. The other thing is that clients hired several students to continue working beyond the scope of the event. Other than that, students got 'swag' and participation credit.

How do you see this kind of experience helping your students with their professional career development, and how does this experience also help them with career preparation?
It helps for a couple of different reasons. They have to use a lot of their soft skills. They're working with a team of graphic designers at different skill levels. So, they're not in their typical class with familiar peers working on the same project. They also have to delegate because you can't get everything done if it's just one person working in seven hours. Some of them also take on leadership roles. As faculty, we always talk about the design process and these freelance opportunities, but a lot of our students don't have many until after they graduate. Through this event, students witness how a design professional navigates that initial interview with a client. This event also adds to a resume by showing what design-related activities students are doing beyond the classroom. The last thing is the event shows students just how powerful design can be, especially within the community. It's one thing for you to create a fictional project, but to actually see it in action is another.

What do you think are the biggest challenges of this kind of experience?
It is a big event, and there are a lot of moving parts. You're coordinating about a hundred people, and don't tell my wife I made this comparison, but it's a lot like planning a wedding. Another challenge we faced is that Blacksburg is a rural college town in southwest Virginia. You don't have as many professional graphic designers as a larger urban city, like Minneapolis or Chicago, would. So I didn't have a huge phone book full of graphic designers I could call up to serve as mentors.

On the flip side, what are the biggest rewards of this kind of experience?
The day of was fantastic. I just loved seeing everything come together—and all the students were excited. But the biggest thing was how, for the last month of classes, the students only talked about DesignUP. Students kept coming up to me and volunteering to be on the executive committee next year.

What advice would you give to students who want to participate in or create this sort of event?
Events like this not only build community and friendships amongst their peers, but I heard from many sophomore students that "I learned an INCREDIBLE amount about ideating and executing ideas from my upper-class peers."

What advice would you give to a faculty member who wants to create a similar event?
First, definitely do it. It is a lot of work, but the reward is huge. And start earlier.

Whatever you're thinking, just add a couple of months. Haha.
Yeah, exactly. The first year, you're going to have a lot of bumps. The second year, you're going to have bumps, but hopefully not as many, and you can start working toward bigger goals. Our number one goal was to create community within our design program. ■

INTERVIEW: *Patrick Finley, DesignUP*

Patrick Finley is a graphic designer and design educator. In 2022, he started DesignUP, which is a philanthropic community giveback design-a-thon that partnered undergraduate graphic design students with professional designers (mentors) and local nonprofits. The inaugural event took place on Saturday, April 2, 2022, on Virginia Tech's Blacksburg campus, and included 52 undergraduate students, 13 student mentors, and 11 nonprofits. The students and mentors were split into 11 teams, with each having (roughly) one member from each undergraduate class being mentored by a professional designer to create various promotional materials for their assigned nonprofit. The materials included redesigned logos, websites, brochures, flyers, and animated mascots.

What made you want to start DesignUP?
I saw this as a way for students to think about design outside of school and as a way to connect with our local community. The structure of the design-a-thon places students into teams with people they don't know. I try to partner freshmen and sophomores with juniors and seniors, which pushes the younger students to elevate their skills and gives the upperclassmen an opportunity to serve as mentors. All of the students benefit from working alongside design professionals and observing how they conduct themselves with clients.

How did you select the nonprofit clients and get their buy-in to participate?
Because it was the first year, we didn't really have a long vetting process. I asked around and was connected with some nonprofits. Additionally, I created some social media posts explaining what we wanted to do for the event. I'd also created a Google client sign-up form. I specified we were looking for nonprofit organizations, but would also consider requests from local small businesses.

Did you have administrative support?
Our dean is always looking for projects that support teaching, research, and service. DesignUP meets all those check-boxes. And our dean had money set aside for outreach activities. The college gave us a little bit more money, as did our department.

So you're saying sometimes people should ask, and you might get lucky with a bit of support.
Exactly. At first, I thought we were going to have to fund raise, and we did try that, but we had struck out. So fortunately the college came through and helped us.

What kinds of roles did the students take on?
All of them were designers, but depending on who their design professional was and what the project was, they acted as more of an advisor. Additionally, a team of students helped with the overall planning. They built the event and created all the promotional materials so that we had sweatshirts, t-shirts, sticker books, notebooks, pens, pencils, and even surge protectors. They were the ones who went to Sam's Club the night before and loaded up two cars full of Gatorade, water, and snacks. They were also the biggest promoters of the event.

It sounds like the students had ownership of this event, but did you do weekly check-ins or anything along the way to ensure that everything was on track?
Yep. We had bi-weekly meetings. We would check-in, and we had a schedule of when we needed everything (printing, t-shirts, sticker books)—so we made sure we were on track.

Chapter 4 key concepts

co-creation: a collective creative activity that is done by more than one person [9]

empathy: the ability to feel what another person is feeling or put yourself in the position of another person

intersectionality: "the ways in which systems of inequality based on gender, race, ethnicity, sexual orientation, gender identity, disability, class and other forms of discrimination 'intersect' to create unique dynamics and effects" [16]

praxis: the process of applying theory to action; enactment or embodiment of ideas

References

1. McCann, Laurenellen. 2019. "The Myth of Everybody." *Medium*. January 22, 2019. medium.com/organizer-sandbox/the-myth-of-everybody-85e4004be1f6; Creative Reaction Lab. 2018. "Equity-Centered Community Design Field Guide."
2. Carroll, Antionette. 2019. "Activism + Impact." Presented at the Latham Lecture, IIT Institute of Design, March 15.
3. Dewey, John. 1933. *How We Think: A Restatement of the Relation of Reflective Thinking to the Educative Process*. Boston: D. C. Heath and Company.
4. Thomas, Joyce, and Deana McDonagh. 2013. "Empathic Design: Research Strategies." *The Australasian Medical Journal* 6 (1): 1–6.
5. Bennett, Cynthia L., and Daniela K. Rosner. 2019. "The Promise of Empathy: Design, Disability, and Knowing the 'Other.'" In *Proceedings of the 2019 CHI Conference on Human Factors in Computing Systems - CHI '19*, 1–13. Glasgow, Scotland: ACM Press.
6. Benson, Eric. 2016. "Designing Sustainable and Equitable Relationships with Communities." In *Developing Citizen Designers*, edited by Elizabeth Resnick, 270–72. New York: Bloomsbury.
7. Maxwell Lane, Marty, and Rebecca Tegtmeyer. 2020. *Collaboration in Design Education*. London, UK: Bloomsbury.
8. Lupton, Ellen. 2017. *Design Is Storytelling*. New York: Cooper Hewitt, Smithsonian Design Museum.
9. Sanders, Elizabeth B.-N., and Pieter Jan Stappers. 2012. *Convivial Toolbox: Generative Research for the Front End of Design*. Amsterdam: BIS Publishers.
10. Bahram, Sina. 2018. "The Inclusive Museum." Prime Access Consulting (blog). October 1, 2018. pac.bz/blog/the-inclusive-museum.
11. Martin, Bella, and Bruce Hanington. 2012. *Universal Methods of Design*. Beverly, MA: Rockport Publishers.
12. Shaughnessy, Adrian. 2010. *How to Be a Graphic Designer Without Losing Your Soul*. Princeton, NJ: Princeton Architectural Press.
13. "Community Engagement." n.d. Carnegie Classification of Institutions of Higher Education. Accessed May 4, 2023. carnegieclassifications.acenet.edu/elective-classifications/community-engagement.
14. "DesignExplorr." 2022. DesignExplorr. July 6, 2022. designexplorr.com.
15. Murdoch-Kitt, Kelly M., and Denielle J. Emans. 2020. *Intercultural Collaboration by Design: Drawing from Differences, Distances, and Disciplines through Visual Thinking*. London: Routledge.
16. "What Is Intersectionality." n.d. Center for Intersectional Justice. Accessed July 11, 2023. intersectionaljustice.org/what-is-intersectionality.

Chapter 5

Finding focus & targeting clients

HOW?

WHO?

WHAT?

WHY?

Once you decide to take on client work in the design classroom, you can determine your focus and target clients with whom you would like to work. Your class or studio may focus on a specific offering, such as graphic design, strategic design, web design, UI/UX, marketing, and advertising. Some classes and studios are cross-disciplinary, while others may focus on a specific mission or social justice. Identifying a focus and understanding value alignments between you and your clients and partners is essential before you begin any project.

This chapter is for both advisors and students who may be taking on leadership roles with client projects. We address framing the scope of projects, the types of clients and partners, and approaches to various contractual arrangements.

Developing design skills

Before we dive in, we should point out that by the time you start working with clients, you will have already taken studio classes to develop your technical and formal skills. Juliette Cezzar's *The AIGA Guide to Careers in Graphic & Communication Design*[1] does a great job of outlining some of the basics of what designers need to know when they start working (see the diagram on page 83). You should already have a solid grasp of typography, image-making, grids, design principles, software, and the basics of clear communication. Some of these skills can be acquired while working with clients or for a student-run agency, but many should be in place before beginning client work.

In addition to visual design, it is necessary to develop communication skills and articulate your ideas through writing and speaking. These skills include everything from one-on-one presentations to larger group presentations. It includes communicating with clients, colleagues, instructors, and outside vendors.

ABOVE

PRISM (Pamplin ReInventing Social Media) students and faculty gather to discuss client work.

RIGHT

Intersection of formal concepts, techniques, methods, and theory (adapted from "The AIGA Guide to Careers in Graphic & Communication Design").

CHAPTER 5: *Finding focus & targeting clients* 85

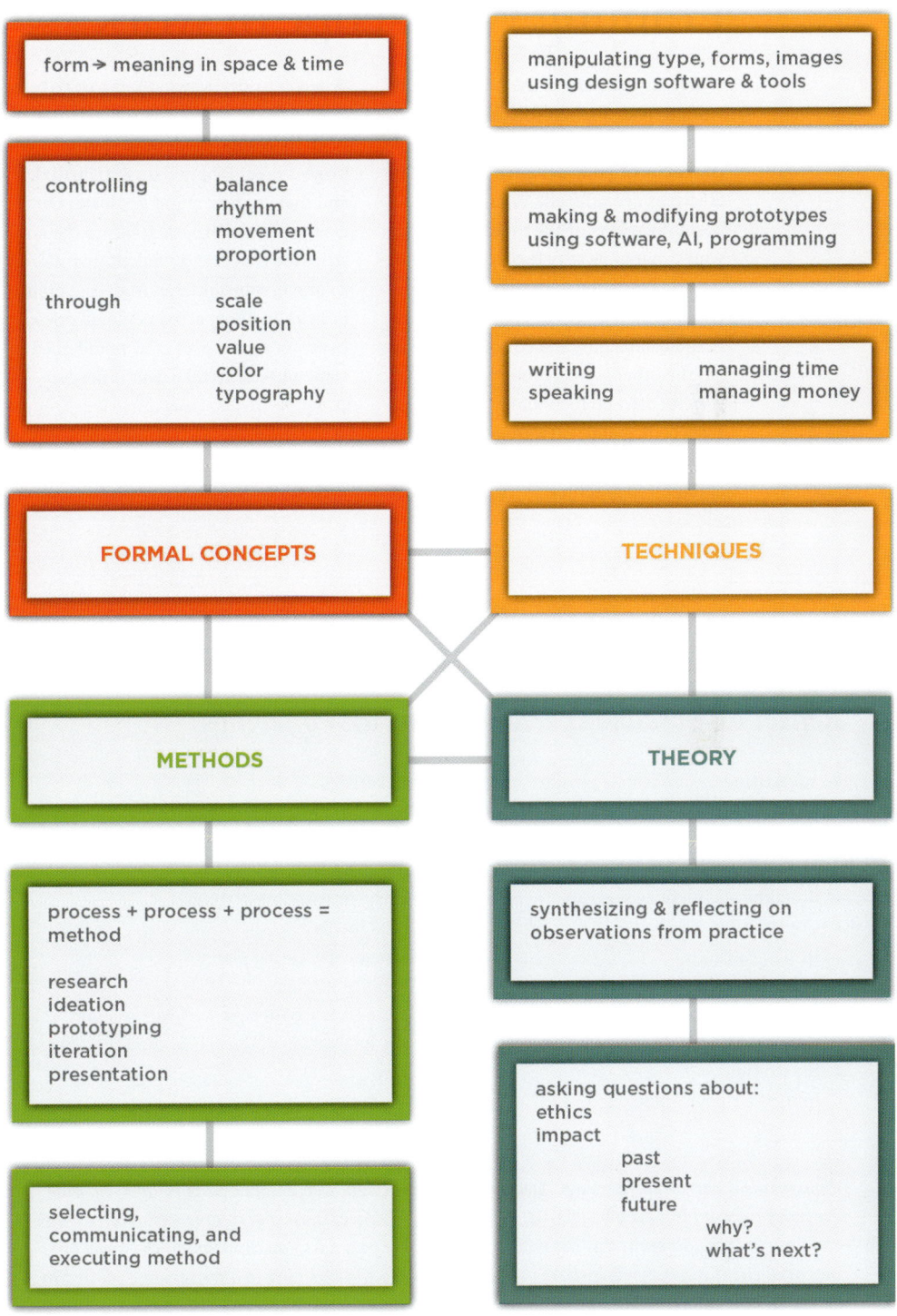

Framing your scope of work

When thinking about the type of client work to take on, first look at the curricular structure of your program. **What is the focus of your design degree? What electives are offered? What are the specializations of the faculty?** Perhaps your program is very focused on branding and typography. In that case, you could work with clients on logo designs, brand campaigns, and editorial systems. On the other hand, if your program is very focused on technology and emphasizes coding and software, you might be more inclined to offer website designs and motion graphics.

When considering what services to offer, don't rely too heavily on the expertise of an individual student. Sometimes, a project takes longer than anticipated, and that student might graduate. Or even when the project sticks to the anticipated timeline, a student might drop a course, transfer to another university, or have an unexpected personal crisis. In any of these cases, you would need someone else to take over if needed.

ACTIVITY 5.1

Reflect on possible specializations and offerings

- Advertising
- Animation
- Augmented reality/virtual reality
- Artificial intelligence
- Branding and identity services
- Copywriting
- Design research
- Editorial design
- Environmental branding
- Eye tracking
- Illustration
- Immersive environments
- Logos
- Marketing
- Posters
- Presentations
- Public relations
- Signage/wayfinding systems
- Social media
- Strategic marketing plans
- Usability studies
- User experience design
- User interaction design
- Video
- Web design
- Web development

Picture this list 10 or 20 years ago. User interaction design, web design and development, and eye tracking wouldn't even be offered. With recent advances in AI and augmented reality, you can imagine how different this list will look in just five years. As you think about the focus of potential client work, consider how you would develop the expertise to offer services related to emerging technologies.

CHAPTER 5: *Finding focus & targeting clients* 87

SURVEY RESULTS

Our design studio provides the following:

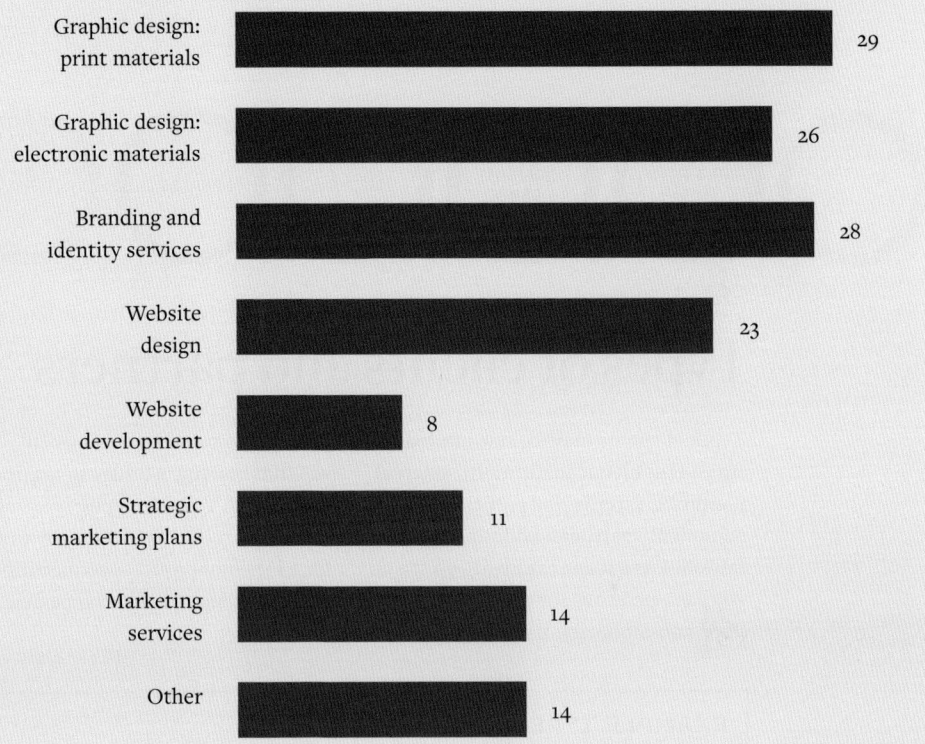

Graphic design: print materials	29
Graphic design: electronic materials	26
Branding and identity services	28
Website design	23
Website development	8
Strategic marketing plans	11
Marketing services	14
Other	14

In 2018, We conducted a U.S. survey of faculty advisors of student-run campus design studios. Here's how the breakdown of work looked then.
What can we imagine it will look like ten years from now?

SCOPE DETERMINES SIZE AND STRUCTURE

Depending on the scale of your class or studio, consider dividing your group into teams. For example, the Capstone Agency at the University of Alabama is structured into six departments with specific functions: [2]

The Capstone Agency assigns a Director and Assistant Director for each department, who then reports back to the Firm Director.

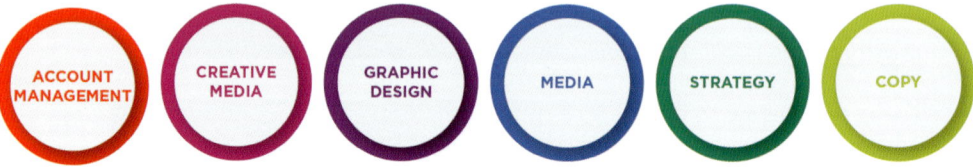

Types of clients and partners

Types of clients may include internal (to your academic institution), external nonprofit, external for-profit, or other community partners. Additionally, if established as a formal student-run studio, you can operate as for-profit, nonprofit, or non-monetary. Each approach provides community engagement, whether building a bridge to a different department across campus, creating a service-learning opportunity by working for a local nonprofit, or connecting students with high-profile companies.

EXAMPLE TYPES OF CLIENTS	
Internal	External
Academic departments *Administrative units* *Student groups*	*For-profit companies* *Nonprofit organizations* *Governmental and civic institutions*

COMPENSATION FOR DESIGN SERVICES

Students and academic programs can be compensated in many ways for their design services. The model you choose will depend on various factors, including your program and institution's size, resources, mission, policies, and local and national regulations.

EXAMPLE TYPES OF COMPENSATION	
Monetary	Non-monetary
Fee-for-service (hourly or flat rate) *Donation to the program* *Scholarship funding*	*No compensation* *Equipment and supply donations* *Event sponsorship*

TO CHARGE OR NOT TO CHARGE?

We will go into more depth on the advantages and disadvantages of charging clients in *Chapter 11: Managing the money*, which focuses on different models that student-run studios can consider. But even if you are dealing with a singular client project, it is worth considering the pros and cons of charging. At first, accepting fees for design services might sound like it has all of the advantages. After all, you'd get money! And with it, all the things money can buy! However, you can quickly get into some sticky territory when you charge a client. Where does the money go? Do you have an account set up to receive funds? Who pays the taxes on the money received? What do you want to do with the money? Will other people come sniffing around once they know money is available?

If you have a client that wants to pay you (or that you want to charge), we recommend reaching out to your program chair or supervisor to get their thoughts. We also recommend contacting your program's fiscal or business manager (if you have one). More often than not, the financial advisor to your program will know more about the particular peculiarities of your institution—or at the very least, they can point you in the direction of someone who does. In some cases, local and national rules and regulations may prevent you from requesting fees for service, or there may be limits on your fee structure.

	Charging	Not charging
Pros	*Money!* *The things money can buy!* *Valuing graphic design*	*No fiscal responsibilities* *Opens up other opportunities*
Cons	*Taxes* *Establishing accounting systems* *Managing money*	*No money* *Overhead expenses unpaid* *Devaluing student labor*

But if you're looking to "try out" paid client work, often, a one-time simple solution can be to ask if a client to simply "make a donation" to the program instead of a payment. While donations still require some paperwork, they often have fewer strings attached than official paid work. Additionally, you can think about if there are other ways of receiving compensation. For instance, would a client be able to donate design books or supplies to your program? Fund scholarships? Sponsor a field trip or agency tour?

RECIPROCAL RELATIONSHIPS

Finally, there are other ways to think about compensation beyond money. After all, clients are also giving you—less experienced designers—their time and attention. Many faculty advisors have the mindset that this is a reciprocal relationship in which students offer their design services while clients provide their energy and resources to bolster student learning. Sometimes, these projects don't end up with tangible deliverables within the constraints of an academic calendar. Any of these approaches are valid as long as you clearly define and articulate your strategy and justification.

FEEDBACK

Clients or community partners can often provide thorough critique and written reflection for students.

Types of clients and partners

You may have taken on client work in the classroom because a client approached your organization. Lucky you! (This excitement assumes that the client seems like a good fit.) But more often than not, you will have to do some legwork to find and keep good clients, especially if your institution is just starting to offer design services. Then, the work of finding clients and partners is ongoing. To begin, you'll want to have a way for clients to contact you. You can create an email specifically for your group or use your faculty advisor's email. Many will also offer a phone number, but someone has to be available to answer the phone professionally and return calls, so this might not be a feasible primary mode of contact. Here are a few ways to find clients:

CONNECTIONS AT YOUR OWN INSTITUTION

One of the easiest places to find client work for students is at your own institution. Many departments could use a rebranding, a new website, some promotional materials, and help with social media—and some will even have a budget to help produce these items. Working within your organization has advantages and disadvantages. It's incredibly convenient to schedule meetings and check out relevant facilities and materials in your own backyard. However, the stakes can be higher when taking on internal clients. For instance, if you redesign your school's website, and the school director or faculty members hate the design, you can be left in an awkward position. But if you can establish clear expectations and good communication throughout the process, you can help avoid such an outcome.

REFERRALS

Word-of-mouth is one of the most common ways of getting new work. Ask around! See if you know anyone who needs design work. Your faculty advisor could email the faculty listserv to inquire if anyone needs design services. Faculty who work on grants may need a little visual help, such as presentations and infographics. Also, once you have a former (happy) client, you can ask them to recommend you. Build it into your process to ask for client testimonials at the conclusion of each project.

COMMUNITY CONTACTS

In *Chapter 2*, we described how Penina Laker at Washington University in St. Louis, Missouri, developed a network of local contacts through community organizations. It's not just faculty who may have great contacts! Poll your fellow students to see who might have connections to a local business or organization.

PUBLIC PRESENCE

If your program has social media accounts, you can leverage these to advertise that you're looking for clients and to specify the kind of work you offer. If you don't have any accounts yet, creating new ones doesn't take too long. But if you do, make sure you plan to keep them populated, and find a good place to store your passwords so future student groups don't have to search for them. You can also utilize your department's website (or create your own) with information about your group.

ADVERTISING

While most advertising requires you to pay, some sites offer free trials or very low-cost advertising. But you don't necessarily need a budget to promote yourself. There might be free ways of advertising through your institution. Could you post a digital ad in a public place on campus? Do you have access to faculty and alumni listservs? Is there a career center that can help? Assess what's already in place and leverage those opportunities.

REQUESTS FOR PROPOSALS (RFP)

You could also respond to RFPs that call for design work and throw your hat into the ring for consideration. The challenge with many RFPs is that they can require a lot of work to apply and can take a long time to get back to you. And there's no guarantee that you will get the job.

INTERVIEW: Brenda Dermody, Technological University in Dublin

Brenda Dermody is a designer, researcher, and lecturer in visual communication at Technological University Dublin, in Ireland. She has a specialized interest in typography and leads design projects across all four years of the BA program. Brenda is also a fellow of the International Society of Typographic Designers and serves on their board. The visual communication design program at TU Dublin is a four-year course of study preparing students for careers in design and for post-graduate research. Engagement with design theory through practice seeks to engender a rich critical understanding of the social, cultural, and technological contexts in which graphic design operates.

Could you describe some of your client-based experiences and their main learning outcomes?

For almost 20 years, I have led students learning with communities through projects in the third year of our BA design program. This stems from my teaching philosophy and my interest in communities of practice. Students spend a lot of their time in college working on hypothetical projects that don't always offer the complexities found in real-life projects. In this context, research findings and design decision-making can be inferred or implicit rather than explicit. Students sometimes focus solely on their own interests within a project, or on what they believe instructors want. I began to feel that there was a real limitation in this approach to learning. By contrast, when you are working on live projects you are negotiating with people who most likely do not have fluency in the visual and verbal language of design. So rather than following an enquiry, you also have to adapt to and incorporate the insights and views of others. This becomes a distinct aspect of the research enquiry and introduces a new set of demands around the communication of research findings and design strategy. It also brings an additional rigor to the development of a visual language. So, I was looking at different ways to introduce live projects. And I felt at the time that the most value would be in working with communities.

How are you initially connecting with these community partners?

Originally, I sourced partners through my own contacts. However, I soon realized that a community partner can reasonably be expected to respond to at most five student presentations or small groups. Higher numbers of students per partner limit meaningful engagement. Since we have 35 students in a cohort, we need to work with several partner organizations each year. We are fortunate that our university has a Students Learning with Communities (SLWC) unit within the Access and Civic Engagement office that has an extensive database of local and national underserved community groups and NGOs who feel that their organization would benefit from students and the university. Every year, I generate a shortlist list of potential partners and meet with colleagues to select several organizations that we feel align with our program learning goals. The SLWC office then contacts the various partners and sets up initial meetings.

From there, we structure the timeframe of the project and set out the parameters. We discuss the terms of the partnership as an equitable exchange where all actors bring their expertise to the table for mutual benefit. The learning agreement states that everyone involved in the research project is entitled to use the outcomes for non-commercial means. So, partners can use the outcomes in presentations and to support funding applications, students receive credits for the module and can feature the work in their portfolios and at job interviews and so on.

INTERVIEW: *Brenda Dermody, Technological University in Dublin*

How do you create equitable practices with engaging students and these partners?
From the outset, I establish a dialogic engagement between partners, students, and the teaching team. We frame the project for students and host an introductory day with the partners who are essentially design clients. We also hold a day at the very beginning of the module to prepare students to meet the partners. We talk about communities of practice, engaged scholarship, and what the partners/clients might bring to the collaboration. We ask the students to reflect on the skills, knowledge, and values they can bring to the project because it's very important that they enter the partnership on an equal footing and with the awareness that they can offer valuable expertise in research and design. This is a key aspect of their learning journey. It gives them confidence to engage in this relationship and produce what will hopefully be useful insights and viable design outcomes for the partners.

What strategies do you use to empower students?
A depth of engagement with research helps students to build their skills in articulating their practice and identifying their own values. Another key skill designers learn is to be comfortable with uncertainty. Every time you begin a new project, it's a step into the unknown. Design projects evolve through dialogue and through iteration. You have to trust in the process.

What are the biggest challenges of this kind of experience?
The biggest challenge is the live nature of the project. Things go wrong—occasionally the project stops or changes direction part way through and the students need to reflect on this and negotiate a new outcome.

What are the biggest rewards of this kind of experience?
Many of the organizations we work with are plugging gaps in community infrastructure: in care, psychological supports, healthcare, education, information, and so on. The community partners are often providing fundamental and necessary services not delivered by systems of government, education, or economy. These organizations are often under-resourced so their day-to-day focus is on keeping the doors open, and keeping operations running. They don't have the time or the budget to buy design expertise. So there's a huge satisfaction for us in being able to work with them to provide that.

What advice would you give to faculty advisors who are interested in doing this kind of experience?
I would say do it! I would say you need to give it time. You need to expect outcomes to be messy. Sometimes the learning isn't in the visual outcomes. One of the things that we do is ask students to do a written reflection at the beginning of the project on how they feel about taking on this kind of work and what their expectations are. And they do a second reflection at the end. We also track the written commentary in their design documents in terms of the research and their own process. Adjusting your project learning outcomes can also make a difference. If your emphasis is on rewarding polished visuals, you might not get that from this kind of project because they are big and sprawling and there is a lot for students to grasp. But if you're open about your learning outcomes and shifting the emphasis towards engagement and process, then you and your students stand to gain a huge amount. ■

ACTIVITY 5.2

DEVELOP A MISSION STATEMENT

A mission statement describes your offerings in a concise narrative. It provides the "why" and "how" of what you do. It serves as a foundation for your business and marketing strategy. Questions to ask yourself as you start thinking about your mission statement:
- What are the desired outcomes of this course/studio?
- What are the skills and talents of the students?
- What are the desires and values of the students?
- What are the desires and needs of your potential clients and partners?
- What makes you unique?

Mission statements

Another part of finding your focus is developing the vision and mission of your collective work. Finding alignment between your client work and the aims of your classroom is an excellent way of articulating the value of your group. Does your school or program have an existing mission statement? If so, does it align with the overall institutional mission statement? How does your client-based course or studio relate to the broader mission?

EXAMPLE: VIRGINIA TECH'S LEARNING OUTCOMES

Institutional level—Virginia Tech's mission: *Inspired by our land-grant identity and guided by our motto, Ut Prosim (That I May Serve), Virginia Tech is an inclusive community of knowledge, discovery, and creativity dedicated to improving the quality of life and the human condition within the Commonwealth of Virginia and throughout the world.*

Program level—Graphic Design program mission: *The mission of the Graphic Design program is to create a community of learning that develops students of integrity, engaged with research and professional practice, in both design and art. The program prepares nimble designers who critically work with their communities in order to identify, frame, and address current cultural issues—as well as envision new hopes for the future. The program strives to reinforce the spirit of Virginia Tech's motto, Ut Prosim (That I May Serve), as a pivotal strategy in a rich design process. Student maturation encompasses 21st-century skills, along with design-thinking competencies, to create leaders in the field across professional practice and academic scholarship.*

Student-run studio level—FourDesign mission: *FourDesign is a collaborative team of student designers, led by industry-experienced faculty, offering a range of talents and fresh perspectives. We value our clients and their expertise as we work together to create strategic, compelling and well-designed branding and marketing communications. We strive to be inclusive and aim to serve our institution and our community by offering quality and researched design services.*

Conclusion

There's much to consider when determining the skills and services you can offer potential clients. While there are a lot of variables, working through the options will help you find the focus of your offerings and determine what kinds of clients and partners would be a good match. Crafting a concise mission statement can help communicate your goals and values to these potential audiences. Ideally, you can develop and sustain reciprocal relationships that are mutually beneficial for everyone involved.

Chapter 5 key concepts

fee-for-service: monetary compensation in exchange for design services

reciprocal relationship: each partner has different needs met through the interaction

RFP (request for proposal): a document that describes a project so that vendors can create estimates and submit for the opportunity to work on it

References

1. Cezzar, Juliette. 2018. *The AIGA Guide to Careers in Graphic and Communication Design.* New York: Bloomsbury Academic.
2. "Capstone Agency." n.d. Capstone Agency. Accessed July 11, 2023. capstoneagency.org.

DEVELOPING CONCEPTS

Virginia Tech students working to develop client designs at the design marathon, DesignUP.

Chapter 6

Achieving learning goals

There are many different approaches to how, when, and where client and community partner experiences happen, from single projects within a class to capstone-level practicum courses, to independent, standalone studios. Each of these approaches is assessed in different ways.

This chapter provides a range of options for how client-based work can be structured within different programs and curricular requirements. We will describe how these projects can be assessed and where they fit into the bigger picture of a design curriculum.

HOW?

WHO?

WHAT?

WHY?

Are we learning?

Once you determine your focus and begin connecting with clients and community partners, you'll need to figure out how you'll know if and what you're learning. We—design educators—develop rubrics and assessment tools to help us discover if learning objectives are being achieved. If we're doing it right, we tell you—our students—about those tools and how they work. Even better, we ask you to co-develop them with us so that you develop more understanding and ownership of your educational journey.

In addition to looking at how client experiences fit within the context of design education, this chapter explores how the programs fit into the university overall, how these projects promote community outreach, and how these professional experiences help create employment opportunities.

> *The first paradigm that shaped my pedagogy was the idea that the classroom should be an exciting place, never boring.*
>
> *If boredom should prevail, then pedagogical strategies were needed that would intervene, alter, even disrupt the atmosphere.*
>
> —*bell hooks,* Teaching to Transgress[1]

Learning with each other

Before we get into the nitty-gritty examples of rubrics and reviews and how to execute them effectively, let's look at the bigger picture of what it means to work together on design teams, just as you would in a real-world workplace context. Research shows that students learn better and are more engaged when they learn together. Collaborative learning leads to improved skills and abilities in critical thinking, intercultural effectiveness, and cognitive behaviors.[2] You're also learning from your clients and community partners, which is more effective in a collaborative environment.[3] In many of these client-based projects, you learn about people with different backgrounds across race, ethnicity, class, culture, income, gender, sexual orientation, ability, religion, and education.

Ideally, a classroom is a space where all feel welcome and where you feel comfortable engaging in debate without fear of retribution. In *Teaching to Transgress,* bell hooks writes that a classroom should be "a place of promise and possibility," through which we resist racist teaching practices and systems.[4] Faculty should offer students the knowledge to "empower them to be better scholars, to live more fully in the world beyond the academy." The classroom should be a place where you can raise critical questions about the learning process and the design industry as a whole.

While you can apply the ideas you learn in school to the rest of your life, directly engaging with clients and communities allows you to use these practices while still protected by the educational environment.

Another aspect of fostering an exciting educational environment is feeling valued and valuing your classmates. Again, bell hooks explains that "as a classroom community, our capacity to generate excitement is deeply affected by our interest in one another, in hearing one another's voice, in recognizing one another's presence." A component of this is acknowledging your own presence and having a self-awareness of your own biases. Everyone brings different perspectives and backgrounds to the classroom, and each individual comes together to build a group dynamic. While a professor plays a vital role in building community, the group forms the feeling of a classroom. Have you ever noticed how a couple of vocal or disinterested students can shift the vibe of a class? Or how a few enthusiastic students make the classroom more exciting and make you want to try harder? To get the most out of your education, actively participate in the learning process.

Defining course- and program-level outcomes

So what does it look like when we combine these ideas about experiential education (which we talked about in *Chapter 1*), standards and outcomes from industry (outlined in *Chapter 2*), and bell hooks' guidance about learning together in a supportive classroom community? As educators, we try to distill all of that into learning outcomes for your degree program and your individual courses. Then, we hold each other accountable on that journey of learning.

Here are some examples of what those outcomes can look like:

Course-level learning outcomes:
- Communicate ideas effectively through the composition of original creative work.
- Exhibit competence with the principles of visual arts and/or design
- Gain professional work experience in the graphic design field.
- Create and develop visual responses to communication problems.
- Illustrate knowledge of tools and technology applicable to area(s) of specialization.
- Develop a portfolio of professional work across a range of project types.
- Understand the attributes and functions of different types of studio structures.
- Articulate the components of the design process in the context of specific projects.

Program-level learning outcomes:
- Create more diverse and inclusive classroom environments through content as well as recruitment of a more diverse student body.
- Engage in experiential learning activities through exhibitions, internships, service learning, and undergraduate research.

Comparing curricular models

CURRICULAR STRUCTURE

Client-based projects can appear in various ways throughout your coursework, from something as small as a single project within an existing class, to something as complex as a student-run, faculty-led studio. These studios can be offered as a class, class/studio, or studio. Additionally, you can operate client projects and studios as for-profit, nonprofit, or non-monetary. The table below outlines some different approaches that you can take.

TYPE	DESCRIPTION	EXAMPLE
Single project in a single course	There is a client-based project within an existing studio class.	Technological University Dublin
Single project across more than one course	There is a client-based project on which students in more than one studio class are collaborating.	University of Arkansas
Practicum class	The entire course is dedicated to client work. This is an upper-level course, possibly a senior capstone course for the program.	*Mint Design Studio* at University of Florida
Student-run agency in class	There is a student-run, faculty-advised agency that operates independently of an existing course.	*FourDesign* at Virginia Tech
Student-run agency outside of class	There is a student-run, faculty- or staff-advised agency that operates independently of an existing course. The agency may operate independently from the semester schedule of the university.	*PRISM* at Virginia Tech *Glyphix* at Kent State

In addition to the options listed here, some institutions allow students to take one of these courses more than once. For example, University of Akron and Ferris State University students take their client-based studio course for a full year. Students at the University of Indianapolis are allowed to take the course up to four times over their final two years in the program.

ASSESSING YOUR WORK

Assessment is vital to working on client and partner projects in a design course. We can't just assume learning is happening; we have to demonstrate it. In *Chapter 3*, Najla wrote about how experiential learning helps you grow and learn as a whole person, not just as a designer. You develop interpersonal skills, communication, teamwork, problem-solving, self-understanding and resilience, leadership, empathy and respect, adaptability, cultural sensitivity, and global citizenship.[5] **Developing these "holistic competencies" is as important as learning knowledge and skills, but they can be hard to assess.**[6] Therefore, we use multiple assessment methods, including reflection and feedback. Below we list some common assessment approaches for client-based projects.

All of these approaches work best when faculty collaborate with students as partners. Students can engage as partners in four key areas of assessment—designing the assessment, establishing grading criteria, self-assessment, and peer assessment.[7]

Common assessment approaches for client-based projects

RUBRICS

Rubrics help clearly communicate the criteria for a successful project. Rubrics also help keep grading equitable—so all students are judged by the same criteria.

EXAMPLE PORTION OF A DESIGN FOUNDATIONS RUBRIC (VIRGINIA TECH)

	0 *Not meeting requirements*	1 *Approaching requirements*	2 *Meeting requirements*	3 *Exceeding requirements*
Communication + Problem solving *Ability to think through a problem or ability to follow a given prompt, develop an innovative solution, and effectively communicate ideas visually*	**No understanding** of assignment. Did not successfully translate work into an appropriate visual form.	**Basic understanding** of assignment. Solution is common or cliché.	Developed creative and original concepts that **fulfill** assignment parameters.	Solutions are distinctive and unique. Projects exhibit the creative thinking process and the development of an individual style. Solutions **go beyond expectations**.
Composition *Application of principles of visual organization, spatial arrangement of individual pieces, use of hierarchy, and implementation of narratives/storytelling*	Composition is **not considered or poorly executed**.	Exhibits a **basic understanding** of spatial arrangement and narratives.	Meets **standard expectations** for spatial arrangement, hierarchy, and use of narratives and storytelling.	**Exemplary** application of spatial arrangement and use of hierarchy to successfully implement storytelling or narratives.
Aesthetics + Technique *Use of color, applied technology, drawing / drafting skills, mark-making, typography, etc.*	Work produced is of **substandard quality**, and is presented in a non-professional manner.	Demonstrates a **basic understanding** of the principles and elements used in the creation of design, and shows potential in the application of selected media. The work is in development.	Demonstrates a solid understanding of the principles and elements used in the creation of design, and exhibits good usage of their selected media. The work shows an **expected quality**.	Exhibits an ideal understanding of the principles and elements used in design, and exhibits excellent usage of the selected media. The work is of **high quality**, and is professionally presented.

PEER REVIEW

In the client-based classroom, faculty might conduct reviews, but you might also have students reviewing one another. This review might take shape as "team leaders" assessing their teams, or you might have "peer reviews" in which all team members complete assessments of one another.

Team leaders might review based on:
- Punctuality/attendance
- Managing deadlines
- Research
- Process work
- Final outcome
- Presentation skills
- Client interaction.

Peer reviews might include questions about:
- Attending working meetings
- Completing assigned responsibilities
- Treating peers with respect
- Overall contributions.

GROUP REVIEW

Most client-based projects happen in groups or teams, so we need to be clear about guidelines for assessing groups. To ensure fairness for gauging individual and collective contributions, you must develop appropriate criteria that everyone understands. Example criteria could include:[8]

- Demonstrates leadership
- Exhibits cooperative attitude
- Applies a variety of methods to deal with different tasks and difficulties
- Engages and stays motivated with the assigned task
- Motivates other people
- Listens and responds to feedback and opinions.

DPC WEEKLY PROGRESS RUBRIC (FERRIS STATE UNIVERSITY)

This example rubric is used to assess progress on the course learning outcome "Professionalism: Ability to prepare efficient meetings, manage updates and vendors, clients. Meeting project milestones, responds to feedback."

Criteria	Excellent: Exceeds expectations for most requirements and grading criteria	Good: Successfully meets most requirements and exceeds expectations in some areas	Average: Accomplishes minimum level of requirements	Poor: Does not meet minimum requirements in some areas

SELF-REFLECTION REVIEW

While most people conduct reviews at the end of a project or the end of a term, giving midterm reviews allows room for students (or faculty) to pivot. A team member might need to realize they are not meeting all expectations or that their grade is being impacted. By providing feedback midway through a course, they can improve before it's too late. Faculty might also consider giving students a midterm review for rating the class, which could offer questions for self-reflection (see below).

Students can also create self-reflection by tracking time and reflective notes through time sheets or tracking software. In another approach, students at Ferris State University complete weekly progress reports to keep track of their progress towards achieving the learning outcome related to professionalism (see the *DPC weekly progress rubric*). These approaches allow students to take ownership of and accountability for their work. They also provide documentation of the project process and an individual's accomplishments. Taking it a step further, students at the University of Indianapolis complete a "process review" at the end of the semester. They document their work in class in a "process book" that can be referenced later on a job interview. It gives you the language and visuals needed to be able to discuss your role and how you collaborated on a group project.

EXAMPLE MIDTERM REVIEW (ANNE H. BERRY, CLEVELAND STATE)

Self-reflection

- I am generally prepared for this class.
- I work hard and offer my best efforts on assignments; I take responsibility for my own learning.
- I take the initiative to talk to the instructor when I have questions or concerns about the class or my work.
- I am an active participant in class and contribute to a positive class environment.
- I make sure I check our class management system (e.g. Schoology, Canvas, Blackboard, Slack) on a regular basis for information about class assignments.
- I am receptive to feedback from my peers.
- I use the feedback I receive from others to improve the quality of my work.
- I am engaged with in-person class meetings.

Instructor feedback

- I find my instructor's feedback to be valuable; my instructor is clear about expectations.
- My instructor takes an interest in my individual progress.
- Provide a brief, general description of any challenges or barriers you are experiencing regarding this course.

Critique and reflection

When dealing with clients, productive critiques (both with a class and with the client) are vital to the overall success of a project. While critiques can be difficult—you poured your blood, sweat, and tears into your work!—they are also the best way to improve. Think of feedback and critiques as opportunities for people to help you succeed.

In Anne H. Berry's typography class at Cleveland State, she printed out a series of questions for reflection and hung them around her classroom. She then asked her students to reflect on each question before hosting a discussion about the value of critique.

In your own words, what is the purpose of critique?

Do you find peer feedback helpful? Why or why not?
Do you use the feedback you receive?

On a scale of 1-5, 5 being very useful and 1 being not useful, provide a rating and explanation for your rating.

Do you find instructor feedback helpful? Why or why not?
Do you use the feedback you receive?

On a scale of 1-5, 5 being very useful and 1 being not useful, provide a rating and explanation for your rating.

Did you make a lot of revisions during the assignment? If so, why? If not, why not?

CHAPTER 6: *Achieving learning goals*

Do you find instructor feedback helpful? Why or why not?
Do you use the feedback you receive?

On a scale of 1-5, 5 being very useful and 1 being not useful, provide a rating and explanation for your rating.

What aspects of the design or critique process do you need to continue getting better at?

When someone makes a comment about your work that you don't like, how do you interpret the criticism? How do you respond? Verbally? Through the process of revision? How does criticism about your work make you feel?

What, if anything, makes it difficult for you to receive feedback about your work?

What are some things you can do to improve your skills when it comes to the critique and revision process?

What, if anything, makes it difficult for you to revise your work?

Conclusion

While it's easy to get distracted by the small fires you must put out in your day-to-day work, try to keep your big learning goals in mind. Reflections and assessments can help you take a step back, view your situation more broadly, and focus on what is most important.

Assessments for client-based work will probably look a bit different than what you're used to in your other courses. They might be more process- or research-focused and are likely more collaborative.

Your faculty advisors are likely providing you with feedback, but remember that they can also benefit from student responses. Giving mid-term and end-of-term feedback will help make your classroom experience better and can help make things better for future cohorts of students.

GIVING BACK

Designer, Kevin Jones of Joba Studio, volunteers his time at a design marathon helping local non-profits.

Chapter 6 key concepts

assessment: evaluating learning within a course, across a series of courses, or across an entire program of study

learning outcome: an intended goal of a course, class, or workshop; framed in terms of what the student will be able to do at the end of the study

rubric: a guide with criteria outlining the required components of an assignment or project; value measurements are attached to each criteria

References

1. hooks, bell. 1994. *Teaching to Transgress: Education as the Practice of Freedom.* London: Routledge.
2. Kilgo, Cindy A., Jessica K. Ezell Sheets, and Ernest T. Pascarella. 2015. "The Link between High-Impact Practices and Student Learning: Some Longitudinal Evidence." *Higher Education* 69 (4): 509–25.
3. Van den Bergh, Marie, Mieke van der Bijl-Brouwer, and Rebecca Price. 2022. "A Community-Based Learning Program to Improve Wellbeing and Design Student Success." In: *Proceedings of DRS2022: Bilbao.*
4. hooks, bell. 1994. *Teaching to Transgress: Education as the Practice of Freedom.* London: Routledge.
5. Weah, Wokie, Verna Cornelia Simmons, and McClellan Hall. 2000. "Service-Learning and Multicultural/Multiethnic Perspectives: From Diversity to Equity." *Phi Delta Kappan*, 673–75.
6. Chan, Cecilia Ka Yuk. 2022. *Assessment for Experiential Learning.* London: Routledge.
7. Ibid.
8. Ibid.

Part three

Who?

CHAPTER 7

Exploring work roles

CHAPTER 8

Establishing relationships

CHAPTER 9

Sustaining relationships

TYPOGRAPHIC TIMELINE

Students from Renée Walker's class working on the Auto-ethnography Typographic Timeline (see more in Activity 1.2)

Chapter 7

Exploring work roles

There are a variety of roles we take on within design teams and projects. In a real-world studio, these roles tend to be fairly straightforward. You're a junior designer, or an art director, or a programmer, and so on. But what happens when you're in a college class where all students are presumably at the same level, looking for the same kinds of learning experiences?

This chapter identifies the responsibilities that students, faculty, and assistants assume and the strategies for dealing with the workload related to those responsibilities. Real-world clients bring real-world challenges. Here, we offer strategies for dealing with conflicts, effectively collaborating, and structuring teams.

HOW?

WHO?

WHAT?

WHY?

Roles for students

Your team roles should reflect the particular specialization of your course topic or studio focus. For instance, if your focus is on web design, your team would comprise different specializations than an advertising-based group. Additionally, the size of your studio would impact the roles or how many students are in each position. And if you're tackling a single client project in the classroom, you would likely have a much more simplified breakdown of responsibilities. You can assign groups—with or without a team leader—or self-select tasks based on the needs at hand.

In many projects, instructors want to provide a similar experience for all students. This can be accomplished by having each student develop initial design concepts. The client chooses one of those concepts (or perhaps a combination of concepts). Then, the student team works together to adapt the chosen concept, and individual students might execute different project elements. This scenario illustrates why it's important to learn to work on someone else's concept. It's an essential skill that will happen again throughout your career.

"I can't tell you how strongly I feel about the experiential learning model. I've seen students blossom and get jobs in a lot of different fields. They're standing out from other students, and they have a narrative."

—Marilyn Jones, Professor Emeritus, Lehigh University, Department of Art, Architecture and Design

CHAPTER 7: Exploring work roles 115

TEAMWORK

Students from Virginia Tech at work during the DesignUP design marathon.

Assigning leaders

At Longwood University, Wade Lough welcomes students as junior designers. Students can take the class up to four times over their junior and senior years, and they can advance to become senior art directors. Wade and his fellow instructors put their trust in their students. They provide a handbook that outlines a code of behavior and the expectations for each position, and the students take it from there. Faculty member Julia Taugner takes a similar approach at the University of Indianapolis. After dividing the students into teams, she assigns a more senior student to the role of art director for each team.

At Glyphix Studio at Kent State University, groups of 2–4 people are mixed up throughout the semester. Advisor Larrie King utilizes this approach to ensure that everyone has at least one leadership role and at least one non-leadership role. Larrie also likes to pair people with different creative processes together so that they can learn from each other.

Finally, some programs create teams without a hierarchy. At Ferris State University, faculty member Alison Popp does not assign project leaders. Instead, she asks one student to be the main communication contact for each client.

Putting teams together

Sometimes, students all take on the designer role, but other times, roles are more clearly distinct and defined as they would be in a design agency. We'll provide a few typical team roles (see the following spread), to help get you started. This scenario is based on the studio at Virginia Tech, which is typically composed of 10–12 students who work with paying clients. Students can participate for class or internship credit, and for this they have standard class meeting times. Additionally, a faculty advisor is dedicated to the studio.

ASSEMBLING EFFECTIVE TEAMS

Team roles

There are all kinds of interesting "personality" tests that can help you reflect on your ways of being and working in the world. In addition, some assessment tools specifically focus not just on your personality but on your personality within a team. Our students have found these tools helpful when strategizing how to distribute work equitably, communicate effectively, create collaboratively, and deal with conflict when it arises. Here are a few that we have worked with successfully:

Belbin Team Roles
Based on research on how people work together, the Belbin Team Roles help people identify the multiple ways they like to work and then apply that to a team. This approach also supports creating diverse teams where people's different skill sets complement each other. There are nine roles in this model: resource investigator, teamworker and coordinator (the "social" roles); plant, monitor-evaluator, and specialist (the "thinking" roles); and shaper, implementer and completer-finisher (the "action" roles).
belbin.com/about/belbin-team-roles

Clifton-Strengths
After an hour-long assessment, you receive a report with your "Clifton-Strengths," including your top five traits. The strengths are categorized into four main domains: executing, influencing, relationship building, and strategic thinking. Once you have your results, the developers encourage users to reflect, to "think about your experiences, your motivations and how you see yourself" and "what you do, how you do it and why."
gallup.com/cliftonstrengths

FourSight model
The FourSight model helps you explore how people think differently when they still need to work together on a team. The four profiles in this model are clarifiers, ideators, developers, and implementers. Surfacing and understanding your differences will help your team function better. The creators of this model believe that their approach will help you discover the strengths of the people on your team, which will increase collaboration, reduce conflict, and help you deliver more effective results.
foursightonline.com/team

Social Change Map
Developed by Deepa Iyer, the Social Change Map offers a social justice-oriented approach to teams and collaborations. This map uses an ecosystem framework with ten roles that many people play when working on social justice efforts: weavers, experimenters, frontline responders, visionaries, builders, caregivers, disrupters, healers, storytellers, and guides. These roles are oriented around equity, liberation, justice, and solidarity values.
socialchangemap.com

FOURDESIGN, VIRGINIA TECH

Studio roles

FourDesign adapts the students' positions based on their individual strengths and the sort of client work they have at the time. All students are expected to attend weekly check-ins and relevant client meetings, and they are required to keep track of their hours (by project) and to regularly backup all work on a server.

Director/Primary Faculty Advisor
- Primary point of contact for the studio
- Handles all initial client screenings, meetings, and procurement of work
- Determines work to be accepted, rejected, or referred elsewhere as deemed appropriate
- Sets creative tone and generates creative briefs for all work assigned to designers
- Attends client meetings
- Assigns projects
- Runs weekly studio meetings and sets agenda
- Provides art direction and technical support for all projects as needed
- Final point of approval on all work leaving the studio
- Faculty member of record (for academic credit), responsible for evaluation
- Final call on staffing decisions
- Serves as the Operations Director (if the studio charges clients)
    - Determines purchasing requests, repairs, and other accounts payable/accounts receivable-related activity
    - Contact person for initial job references and requests
    - Representative of the studio for presentations and lectures about the studio
    - Provides fiscal reports
    - Sets budgets, confirms rates through annual rate review
    - Generates an annual report of activities.

Secondary Faculty Advisor
- Attends studio meetings as deemed necessary by the Director/Primary Faculty Advisor
- Provides art direction, feedback, and technical support in their respective areas of expertise
- May be assigned specific projects as a Project Manager at the discretion of the Director
- Meets with staff as needed to provide guidance on studio projects
- Attends relevant client meetings and presentations as deemed necessary by the Director
- Provides input on final evaluations (grades) and hiring or firing decisions as needed.

Graduate Assistant
- Dedicates hours to the studio
- Serves as a point of contact for client communication, prospects, etc.
- Sometimes oversees given projects as deemed appropriate for the benefit of the team
- Meets with staff as needed to provide guidance on studio projects
- Provides input on final evaluation (grades) and hiring or firing decisions (as appropriate).

Student Manager
- Sets student/intern work schedules each term
- Forwards agenda item requests from team to Director
- Generates and maintains team member and vendor contact lists
- Oversees staff duties
- Maintains records of current assignments
- Coordinates with project leads and point persons
- Generates job jackets and status sheets for new work based on information provided by the Director
- Ensures that incremental and final backups are being made of all work
- Responsible for final job close-out procedures (archiving work, etc.)
- First point of student contact for grievances
- Acts as second in command when the Director is not present
- Reports any studio issues promptly to the Director
- Performs other tasks as assigned by the Director.

Graphic Designer/Web Designer/Social Media Specialist
- Brainstorm and sketch on assigned projects as deemed necessary
- May serve as a point person on assigned projects
- May serve as a special team member as assigned
- Revises selected work, including all production required to take a project to completion
- Presents work to client as requested
- Regularly maintains website and social media.

Programmer
- Regularly makes updates to website (if the studio has a website)
- Manages hosting
- Coordinates with Student Manager and Web Designer.

AI Specialist
- Keeps current with trends in artificial intelligence (AI)
- Explores possibilities with AI + code/images/video/copy
- Applies ethics, fair use, and transparency of sourcing.

Photographer
- Coordinates with Web Designer and Programmer to update website with photography
- Goes on photo shoots for select client work
- Presents work to client as requested
- Coordinates with Student Manager and point persons on projects
- Ensures all images are color-corrected and are the proper type (CMYK for Print, RGB for Digital), file format, and resolution
- Ensures that an organized backup of all photographs are housed on the server
- Documents completed projects.

SWOOP (STUDENTS WORKING ON OUR PROFESSION) AGENCY

University of North Texas's student-run advertising agency roles:

Account Executive
The Account Executive (AE) is the face of SWOOP to the client. They manage the account budget, client pitches, meeting scheduling, and they relay information to the account team. The AE is at the top of the chain of command—all work must first be presented to the Account Executive to ensure it aligns with the client's expectations.

Account Planner
The Account Planner is the consumer's advocate throughout the process of developing a campaign or promotion. They conduct consumer research and develop a brief to guide the creative team in constructing their advertisement. To do so, the planner must distill all important information about the consumer and their product into a single idea.

Art Direction
Art Directors are responsible for the visual execution of ad campaigns throughout various media. They are intrinsically creative and should be well-versed in design, visual storytelling, strategy, and necessary software, such as Adobe Creative Suite. Art Directors are paired with copywriters to produce ads and promotional tools that fulfill the client's goal.

Copywriting
Copywriters are the creative writers behind magazine ads, billboards, commercials, and other promotional tools. The writers collaborate with the Art Director to create original content that promotes a product or service to achieve the client's goal. Copywriters need to be experts in grammar, punctuation, and spelling to properly proofread all work the agency produces.

Social Media
Social Media Managers are experts on all social media platforms. They are in charge of integrating campaigns to fit social media and monitoring all activity on said media. The success of their social media campaigns is measured by analytics, engagement, shares, followers, and many more parameters. To be successful, SM Managers must stay up-to-date with current trends across platforms to keep their clients relevant in the eyes of the consumer.

Media
Web Designers and Videographers are an agency's unsung heroes behind the scenes. They build and maintain the infrastructure of SWOOP and without them, the agency would crumble like a stale cookie.

Exploring career possibilities

As discussed in *Chapter 3: Becoming empowered*, developing a sense of agency and purpose, along with opportunities to engage in your community while receiving mentorship, can help empower you during your transition to adulthood. Not only do student-run studios and client jobs foster such developmental milestones, but they are also a great way to try various career roles.

The teams typically formed for client work in the design classroom are similar to those at most firms. (See the following spread for a graphic based on common design positions, adapted from one by Juliette Cezzar, in her book *The AIGA Guide to Careers in Graphic & Communication Design*).[1]

For instance, you might learn that you love coding and troubleshooting and prefer that to front-end development. Or you might take on the role of Art Director and discover you have a knack for project direction and bringing out the best in people. Conversely, you could discover there's a task you despise, which can be just as valuable as finding out what you enjoy. Maybe you always loved drawing, but when you worked as an illustrator for a client, you didn't like making multiple revisions and altering your style to fit the client's wishes. By discovering these insights while in the safety of an educational environment, you can enter the workforce with a clearer path in mind.

Roles for instructors

Instructors take on many roles in managing client work or a student-run design firm. They must hire and manage students (or at least oversee the process), deal with logistics, find their teaching style, and balance their responsibilities with the rest of their workload. Some faculty members have a reduced course load because of their involvement with student-run agency activities, or they run a studio-based course as a part of their regular teaching load. For other faculty members, their only responsibility is managing a studio. On the opposite end of the spectrum, some faculty members receive no course reduction and take on the extra duties in addition to everything else. While there's no one way to handle client work in design education, the more support faculty have from their institutions, the more an organization can thrive.

THE ART DIRECTOR VS. MENTOR/COACH

Of the many student-run centers and courses we have observed, we have seen two primary management styles among instructors: the "Art Director" and the "Mentor." The Art Director approach is where the instructor manages client work much like in a regular studio. They provide direction, have the final say in decisions, and manage students much like in many traditional "real world" studios where students can be fired from projects or told to approach a solution in a certain way. This model heavily emphasizes learning-by-doing, where the learning is tacit and implicit. The instructor works alongside students, emulating standards of practice.

The Mentor method provides counsel to students, but also gives them more autonomy in the decision-making process. This approach is more similar to an empowered design classroom environment, where time is spent teaching and letting students explore. While most faculty end up with a hybrid between Art Direction and Mentorship, we encourage any model that best supports students' development and their path to empowerment. However, we also understand that it can be difficult to "let go" of control, particularly when it comes to high-stakes or high-dollar clients—but taking on the role of mentor doesn't necessitate an entirely hands-off approach either. However, we encourage the perfectionist advisors (faculty or students) to be mindful of how much they control the final output.

By focusing on framing project activities and goals, instructors, and students can develop an optimal balance of control and freedom. Instructors can ask you to collaboratively set goals and ground rules for the projects. Then, when they give you specific instructions, they tell you why they're asking you to do it that way. Instructors should explain the methodologies you're using—the what, why, and how you're using tools and methods like briefs, drafts, and critiques. This connects back to the metacognition and reflection-in-action we talked about in *Part 1*.

ON THE RIGHT

Common positions in design firms and agencies (adapted from Juliette Cezzar's "The AIGA Guide to Careers in Graphic & Communication Design"

CHAPTER 7: Exploring work roles

EXECUTIVE CREATIVE DIRECTOR ······· owner/founder
head of design
chief creative officer

CREATIVE DIRECTOR
······· design director
design manager
product manager

ASSOCIATE CREATIVE DIRECTOR

related mid-level
(non-design):
copywriter
front-end developer
marketing coordinator
media planner
production coordinator
project manager
public relations
social media manager
stragetist
web producer

ART DIRECTOR

SENIOR DESIGNER

MID-LEVEL DESIGNER ·······
content strategist
design strategist
exhibition designer
experience designer
information architect
information designer
interaction designer
package designer
product designer

JUNIOR DESIGNER ·······
AI specialist
design assistant
digital designer
graphic designer
interactive designer
junior art director
junior motion designer
production designer
UI/UX designer
visual designer
web designer

INTERN

Common positions in design firms and agencies

Dealing with disagreements

Your team is built from artists and designers. They are likely independent, strong-willed, and passionate about what they do. Like most creative groups or large extended families, they aren't always going to agree or even get along all the time. But it is important to maintain an atmosphere of mutual respect for clients, directors, and fellow team members. When grievances or disagreements arise and cannot easily be resolved among peers, students should reach out to the faculty advisor to help resolve the conflict. Avoid rumors, backtalk, and any additional unprofessional behavior, as it creates an unproductive, negative working environment for everyone.

SOCIAL CONTRACTS

You might consider posting a "code of conduct" or "principles of community." You can get ahead of many issues by addressing the fact that the team will have disagreements and differences of opinion (and by talking about how to treat each other with respect during these times) before conflict arises.

Your institutions might already have codes of conduct or community principles in place. Not only will it save you some effort to use what your institution has already created, but you will also know that your larger organization backs you up. For instance, Virginia Tech has a publicly posted principles of community:

- We affirm the inherent dignity and value of every person and strive to maintain a climate for work and learning based on mutual respect and understanding.
- We affirm the right of each person to express thoughts and opinions freely. We encourage open expression within a climate of civility, sensitivity, and mutual respect.
- We affirm the value of human diversity because it enriches our lives and the University. We acknowledge and respect our differences while affirming our common humanity.
- We reject all forms of prejudice and discrimination, including those based on age, color, disability, gender, gender identity, gender expression, national origin, political affiliation, race, religion, sexual orientation, and veteran status. We take individual and collective responsibility for helping to eliminate bias and discrimination and for increasing our own understanding of these issues through education, training, and interaction with others.
- We pledge our collective commitment to these principles in the spirit of the Virginia Tech motto of *Ut Prosim* (That I May Serve).

ACTIVITY 7.1

Develop a community agreement

You can work as a team to develop a community agreement—and in fact, this is a good annual exercise to ensure that you are addressing the current needs of your group.

To do this, set aside an hour with your team. Spend the first 10–20 minutes having every individual write what comes to mind for the following:

Blue sky scenario—What do you want from this community/experience? (E.g., getting to work with clients, giving back to our community, working on presentation skills.)

Community assumptions—Describe the conditions of your environment (E.g., what kind of institution are you affiliated with?, what are the backgrounds of the stakeholders?).

Community guidelines—Consider best practices and behaviors (E.g., treating one another with respect, prioritizing clear communication, being mindful of each other's time).

Then, compile everyone's responses into a shared document and discuss the responses. Try to combine similar answers, but make sure everyone's voice is heard.

A NOTE ON PROFESSIONALISM

Be mindful that "professionalism" can be interpreted differently based on culture and background—so be respectful of individual choices (such as hairstyles) and be mindful of circumstances (e.g., not everyone can easily afford a new suit to wear to a client meeting).

That said, when you're working with clients, you want to conduct yourself professionally and respectfully. For instance, consider the following:
- Be attentive during meetings (no cell phones, zoning out, etc.).
- Be mindful of deadlines. If you don't think you can meet a deadline, let your professor or studio director know as soon as possible so they can work to find someone else to complete the task.
- Don't be late.
- If you make a mistake, own up to it. Apologize for what you've done wrong and make changes to ensure that you won't make the same mistake in the future.
- Use email etiquette. Address and sign emails, proofread, and include relevant information.
- Be honest and ethical.
- If you decide to quit, give as much notice as possible. While you often hear of giving two-week notice at jobs, the more time you can give, the better. Also, remember that in this environment, you might have to have the faculty member for another class.

Applying for the client-based experience

Many client-based programs require that students apply to participate. Typically, this is similar to applying to any other internship or job, where you need to submit the following:
- cover letter
- resume
- portfolio or work samples

If you pass the initial review, you may also need to come in for an interview. In most cases, the instructor will conduct the interview. Sometimes more senior-level students will conduct interviews, either to hire their replacement or to hire their team.

If you're either tasked with interviewing someone or prepping for an interview, consider the following questions/prompts:
- Describe your creative process.
- How do you respond when a client gives you negative feedback?
- Describe a time when you collaborated.
- Do you work well in teams? If so, what role have you played?
- Are you good at meeting deadlines?
- What makes you want to be a part of this organization?
- What is your biggest strength?
- What is your greatest weakness?
- Describe the process behind this portfolio piece.
- What do you currently know about this organization?
- Do you have any questions for us?

While we understand the need for some programs to limit the students who can participate in these experiences, we encourage you to center equity as part of these application and evaluation processes.

Conclusion

Any chance you get to try out different work roles will give you insight into what sort of work you want to do after graduation. Working with clients while in the safety of the classroom gives you insights about work environments that you might not get in a typical class (and also gives you a good resume booster).

Suppose there's a particular skill you're interested in developing. In that case, you can always ask your advisor if they'd be willing to let you work in that area (whether you want to take on a leadership responsibility or try your hand at a particular field like advertising or motion graphics). And remember that learning what you *don't* like is as valuable as discovering what you love doing.

Chapter 7 key concepts

art director: leader of a design project; may assign tasks, guide and approve designs, and/or choose thematic direction and imagery

framing: a process in design used to develop a point of view on the specific problem, need, or want of the client or customer

professionalism: the competence and expected behaviors and skills of someone in the workplace; often used in reference to "soft" skills

social contract/community agreement: an agreement co-created among team members that specifies how people will behave and communicate

References

1. Cezzar, Juliette. 2018. *The AIGA Guide to Careers in Graphic & Communication Design.* New York: Bloomsbury Academic.

CASE STUDY: Arsaga's Coffee, University of Arkansas School of Art

Dina Benbrahim and Ryan Slone teach at the University of Arkansas. Dina is a Moroccan multidisciplinary creative who uses an intersectional feminist lens to investigate design for visibility, civic action, and social justice for minority communities, to reimagine equitable futures collectively. Ryan is a designer and educator whose work focuses on social-advocacy poster design, speculative processes, and constraint-led provocations.

They collaboratively taught an Identity Design course, through which they had students brand a new Arsaga's Coffee, which was being constructed in their School of Art building. Arsaga's Coffee Roasters is a small, family-owned business located in the Ozark Mountains of Northwest Arkansas. Their purpose is to bring you great coffee in a warm atmosphere, to create a communal experience, and to give back to the community by empowering people to realize the work they care about doing.

CLIENT: Arsaga's Coffee
COURSE: Identity Design, University of Arkansas (undergraduate)
PROJECT LENGTH: 8 weeks

Third-year students across two sections spent half of a semester creating a brand for a new location of Arsaga's Coffee. The company brand has its own atmosphere and spirit for each new location. However, when the students conducted their initial research, they noted that while each location is different, the brand remains inventive, artsy, quirky, and eclectic, with a solid emphasis on typography.

The client requested a menu, coffee packaging, and practical applications. However, the faculty also encouraged students to be speculative and produce the "dream deliverable" in which students could imagine a thematic package. Eight groups comprised of three students each presented client solutions.

CENTRAL RESEARCH QUESTION
What kind of experience do we want for Arsaga's at the School of Art and how can these students imagine it together collaboratively?

CASE STUDY: Arsaga's Coffee, University of Arkansas School of Art

SCHEDULE

Week 1:
Introduce project
Meet at Arsaga's
Discuss creative brief

Week 2:
Research
Progress meetings

Week 3:
Work time
Speculative deliverable and menu draft critique

Week 4:
Refine and build deliverables
Progress critique

Week 5:
Refine and build presentation

Week 6:
Critique with client
Group feedback

Week 7:
Work time
Client response

Week 8:
Final presentations

AUDIENCE
University of Arkansas students and faculty (with a focus on art, design, and architecture), Arsaga's staff, members of our local community in Fayetteville, visiting artists and speakers.

OBJECTIVES
Design a strong visual system for Arsaga's new location that translates easily across different media, and actively collaborate with design, ceramics, and fabrication teammates to manifest a cohesive series of work.

TONE
Inviting, welcoming, communal, not institutional, quirky.

CASE STUDY: Arsaga's Coffee, University of Arkansas School of Art

MANDATORY DELIVERABLES
+ Inspiration moodboard
+ Menu
+ Special, limited edition coffee packaging
+ Slides to present your work to Arsaga's.

RECOMMENDED DELIVERABLES
+ Bike carrier branding
+ Environmentals
Think about how you would envision the audience experiencing the built environment—examples could be indoor (digital or built) signage, wall and floor graphics, displays, etc. They could be informational, directional, or simply fit within your design system.

     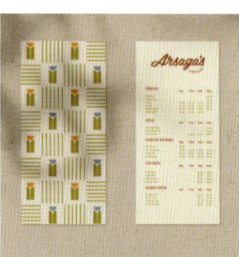

When the students presented their work for class feedback, Dina and Ryan set the following ground rules:
1. We don't judge or label the person or group presenting. We are work-focused.
2. We believe in feedback that is constructive and beneficial to the process.
3. We welcome all thoughts but are mindful of everyone's time, so we'll limit feedback to 3–5 min after each group presents.
4. We encourage everyone to take notes and offer their thoughts.

The agenda for their progress critique was three-fold:
1. Each group will present, one at a time, and describe their overall theme.
2. We'll look at process, logo iterations, brand assets (color, type, iconography, etc.), menu design, coffee packaging, and additional deliverables.
3. There are a lot of options, with a multitude of different ideas and solutions. Making decisions like this takes time, so we hope today is marked by conversation as opposed to final decisions.

CASE STUDY: Arsaga's Coffee, University of Arkansas School of Art

INTERVIEW WITH DINA BENBRAHIM AND RYAN SLONE

Jessica and Meaghan interviewed Dina and Ryan about the experience. Here are a few takeaways:

ON GRADING:

Dina: Feedback is more important than a grade. And I think Ryan and I align on this. We gave constant feedback—pretty much every single session. So there is never really a surprise on how things are going. I think it's just about coming to class and showing up and doing the work and trying your best. I don't think it's about grading how the craft looks because they're still learning. And I think grades don't mean anything when you graduate unless they're going for a master's degree.

BIGGEST CHALLENGES:

Dina: One of the biggest challenges was preparing and trying to organize as much as possible before meeting the students. We were also supposed to collaborate with ceramics and fabrication sculpture students and professors. We had all these questions we didn't have answers to, but we still had to make it somewhat organized for the students so they wouldn't feel completely freaked out. So, one thing we did early on was organize all these thoughts in a brief, similar to a project description.

Ryan: We had pressure and expectations. We were working with this established, well-respected local business that has been such a landmark spot in Fayetteville for 30-plus years. We didn't want to screw this up. There's a lot on the line—relationship-wise—with people within the institution and that family. And I was really overwhelmed and anxious, in part because we didn't even know what the physical space was going to look like.

BIGGEST REWARDS:

Dina: It's all about seeing students' processes evolve and them trying new things and taking risks—and seeing them having fun and having conflicts and solving them. All these real-life things that happen outside the classroom. It wasn't just an imaginary project; it was something real and tangible that was brought up in a client setting. But it was also rewarding to see how they interacted with each other and with Ryan. I think that's the most beautiful part—that relationship part.

Ryan: I connected with some of these students in that class specifically because we went through a challenge together. You feel closer to someone. As they graduate, I became really close with a few of them, and there's that level of trust because we've worked so closely together. Building that relationship was really important. I've also enjoyed literally being in the space and seeing how Arsaga's has impacted the School of Art. Seeing how Arsaga's has become a focal point for this collective of artists, of designers, of people within the community.

One team even proposed a name change from Arsaga's to Artsaga's, due to the proximity to the art school.

SAY CHEESE!

Photo shoot with PRISM (Pamplin ReInventing Social Media) students from Virginia Tech.

Chapter 8

Establishing relationships

The best way to build and maintain strong relationships is to establish clear communication. Designers should listen to clients and be able to articulate and confirm expectations. They should also develop knowledge and skills in project management and financial management, including analyzing and creating contractual documents (more on this in Chapter 11: Managing the money) *and creative briefs.*

This chapter uncovers the nuts and bolts of establishing relationships and beginning to work with clients and community partners. We will also share advice for project management and scheduling.

HOW?
WHO?
WHAT?
WHY?

Understanding the client

There are three main kinds of clients in the design classroom: internal (to your school), external nonprofit organizations or institutions, and external for-profit businesses (albeit there are additional paths to external collaboration, such as community partnerships or collaborations with nonprofits). Each provides community engagement, whether it is building a bridge to a different department across campus, creating a service learning opportunity by working for a local nonprofit, or connecting you with high-profile companies.

Whenever possible, try to work with people who understand that working with a student group isn't the same as hiring a large-scale design firm. While most student groups can produce high-quality work that will fulfill a client's needs, this is not the only goal of the interaction. For instance, if a client isn't happy with a design direction, your group might ask the client to explain their thoughts so you can better learn from the experience. Additionally, many institutions will ask clients to complete an exit survey, information from which can further help students grow from each interaction. Remember that the ultimate goal of client work is to be an experiential learning opportunity. If clients do not value you or your work, the faculty or advisor might need to step in to advocate for student needs.

No matter who the client is or whether or not you are getting paid, you must understand their expectations and communicate clearly. Additionally, you need to have a fee structure in place and be able to provide estimates, invoices, and timesheets. Even if you aren't charging fees for your work, it's still a good idea to give written confirmation of what services will be provided and how many hours will be dedicated to the project.

INITIAL MEETINGS

You'll want to set up an initial meeting once you are ready to start working with a client. The first point of contact might be with a faculty advisor, but ideally, students get to participate in the process early on. Whenever you schedule a meeting with a client, clearly articulate the purpose of that meeting. State what you hope to accomplish during your time together. At this "getting to know you" meeting, you'll want to ask a lot of questions and take notes on what you hear. **Good designers are curious. The more you can learn about your client and their needs, the better.** (See *Questions and prompts to ask clients* to help get you started.) One of our favorite things about being designers is that we're continually learning about different industries and the world around us via the array of clients we work with.

CHAPTER 8: *Establishing relationships* 137

INTERACTING WITH CLIENTS

Questions and prompts to ask clients

You can tailor these based on the specifics of each project. For example, you'd want to ask questions related to a brand campaign, website design, or advertising project if that was the project scope.

- Tell me a bit about your company.
- What are you most proud of?
- What is your goal for the future of the company (or with this design)?
- What adjectives would you use to describe your organization?
- What design services are you looking for? (Ideally you'll already have a rough idea before the initial meeting, but it's still a good idea to clarify.)
- What is your time frame?
- Who are your primary competitors? What sets you apart?
- Is there a problem you're trying to solve? If so, how would you frame that problem?
- Are there any companies you admire?
- Do you have any established brand colors? If not, do you have any colors in mind (or any colors that you hate)?
- Printing/production clarifications (e.g., Who is printing the brochure (and do you need us to manage printing?) Who is coding the app/website (and how would we communicate with them, or do you want us to code the website?)?).
- Is there anything else you'd like us to know?

At the end of the meeting, we recommend summarizing what you heard and repeating it back to the client to ensure you're on the same page. Before you conclude the meeting, you'll want to make sure you have established:

1. the scope of work
2. the general time frame and any important milestones or deadlines
3. enough information about the project to start the design process.

It's also helpful to schedule the next meeting during that first meeting to avoid having to go back and forth via email a dozen times. Scheduling moves quickly when everyone can check their calendars together in real-time. However, you might have to check with your team or other client projects before confirming your availability. If that's the case, make sure you follow up promptly.

Creative briefs

Following an initial client meeting (or two), design teams then develop a creative brief based on meeting notes, interviews, readings, and discussions between the client and the design team. The brief is created and shared with the client before any work begins. This brief is ideally created on student projects in collaboration between the students, instructor, and client.

A brief usually serves the following functions:
- Communicates the beginnings of the creative solution
- Provides an overall framework for the creative approach
- Emphasizes crystallizing strategic ideas to provide a springboard to inform and inspire creative ideas
- Functions like a map leading towards the solution
- Continues to inform and guide the work throughout the project.

A good creative brief will answer these questions:
- What is this project?
- Who is it for?
- Why are we doing it?
- What needs to be done? By whom? By when?
- Where and how will it be used?

There are a lot of different approaches to the brief itself, but you can generally expect to see certain elements within it. See *What to includ in a creative brief* on the next page for a general template.

The creative brief is used at the start of a project and throughout the entire creative process. It is the one element that has been agreed upon and acts as a shared guideline. Clients use it to organize and develop consensus within their enterprises. Then, they use it to help determine if the creative has solved the problem as intended.

BASICS OF CREATIVE BRIEFS

What to include in a creative brief

1. Background summary
- Who is the client?
- What is the product or service?
- What are the strengths, weaknesses, opportunities, and threats (or SWOTs) involved with this product or service?
- Can existing research, reports, and other documents help you understand the situation?

2. Overview
- What is the project?
- What are we designing and why?
- Why do we need this project?
- What's the opportunity?

3. Drivers
- What is our goal for this project?
- What are we trying to achieve?
- What is the purpose of our work?
- What are our top three objectives?

4. Audience
- Who are we talking to?
- What do they think of us?
- Why should they care?

5. Competitors
- Who is the competition?
- What are they telling the audience that we should be telling them?
- Do we have/need a SWOT analysis (strengths, weaknesses, opportunities, threats) on them?
- What differentiates us from them?

6. Tone
- How should we be communicating?
- What adjectives describe the feeling or approach?

7. Message
- What are we saying with this piece exactly?
- Are the words already developed, or do we need to develop them?
- What do we want audiences to take away?

8. Visuals
- Are we developing new images or picking up existing ones?
- If we create them, who/what/where are we photographing or illustrating?
- And why?

9. Details
- Any mandatory information that must be included?
- List of deliverables? Preconceived ideas? Format parameters?
- Limitations and restrictions?
- Timeline, schedule, budget?

10. People
- Who are we reporting to?
- Who exactly is approving this work?
- Who needs to be informed of our progress?
- By what means?

140 CHAPTER 8: *Establishing relationships*

EXAMPLE PROJECT BRIEF

Interpreting Constitutional Amendments

In this project, instructor Annabelle Gould provides the following brief and works with students to develop a poster over the course of three weeks.

PROJECT BRIEF

Design a poster representing one of the 27 amendments to the U.S. Constitution. Your poster can remind people of the amendment's original purpose and importance, raise awareness about a particular issue related to the amendment, or call for a change to the amendment itself. Plenty of high-profile issues in the news now directly relate to some amendments: freedom of religion, freedom of speech, freedom of the press, the right to keep and bear arms, and the right to vote, to name a few. Your audience is college students on this campus.

LEARNING OBJECTIVES

- Integrate text and image using the four methods described in the book *Type, Image, Message* by Skolos + Wedell.
- Recognize the design opportunities that come with using type as an image.
- Work in large scale, and encourage the viewer to engage with the poster from various distances.

DELIVERABLES

- One 16 by 22-inch poster, printed in color
  (text from the selected amendment must be included)

  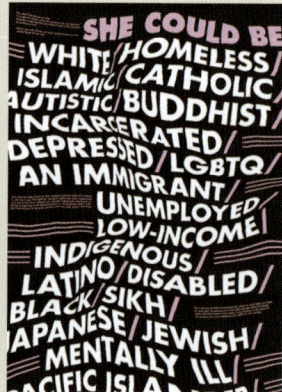

Left: *Isaac Jaeger | Guns + the Second Amendment*
Middle: *Jacob Etelamaki | States Rights + the 10th Amendment*
Right: *Andrew Le | Voting + the 19th Amendment*

Faculty: *Annabelle Gould*
Source: *teachingresource.aiga.org/project/interpreting-constitutional-amendments*

Developing meaningful relationships

Trust, respect, and clear communication are some of the most important components of developing and maintaining good client relationships. If you agree to complete a project by a specific date, do your best to meet deadlines. If you can't, make sure that you communicate the delay to your client well before the due date.

Another aspect of communication is accessibility. Team leaders must be available (within reason—you don't need to be taking phone calls at 10pm) and approachable. Do both clients and your team feel comfortable talking with you? You'll also want to be professional. How do you answer the phone? Have you considered how your voicemail message sounds to others? Do you always address emails to the sender and proofread your messages? Learning how to communicate effectively with clients in a service relationship is critical to your education journey.

Clients also need to fulfill their end of the bargain. They need to make decisions promptly and in a unified voice by identifying who is making the decisions. They need to provide you with any content that is necessary in order to complete the work. This might include completing a brand questionnaire or providing photographs and copy for a website.

One of the hardest parts of a client relationship is handling negative client feedback. What happens when the client doesn't like the work? You want to learn from this experience, so ask follow-up questions if a client isn't satisfied. Encourage your clients to be honest and direct, but remember there's a difference between giving a negative critique and being a jerk. Tone matters. Unfortunately, some clients will talk-down to students. But **a good client will provide you with explanations, articulate their thought process, and treat you with respect, even when they aren't satisfied with your solutions.** In turn, you should always treat them respectfully, even when you're upset by their choices or feedback.

Responding to client feedback

When you start working with clients, it can be challenging to guide client feedback so that you get the information you need in order to change and improve your design. Sometimes feedback is vague or confusing—"I was hoping for something different." Sometimes the feedback is clear—"I don't like that"—but it doesn't necessarily help you figure out the next steps. It doesn't mean the client is difficult; it just means they might need some guiding questions to help you collectively determine the path forward. Here are some typical responses we've heard from clients over the years, with corresponding follow-up questions to keep the conversation moving.

> I don't like that.

>> Can you be more specific about what it is you don't like? Is it the colors, the typeface, the imagery?

> I was hoping for something different.

>> Can you say more about that? What part of the design isn't quite what you were imagining?

CHAPTER 8: *Establishing relationships* 143

> I just don't like that color.

> I understand. We chose that color for _____ reasons. Is there another color that you think could also evoke those ideas?
>
> Note: Sometimes we ask clients *before* we begin if there are any colors they hate (or that their competitors use) or any colors they would like us to use because of existing brand systems.

> Can we make everything brighter and bigger?

> We change some things, but we also want to maintain visual hierarchy—not everything can be big and bright, or people won't know what to look at first. It's important to retain some negative space and variation to lead the viewer through the design.

> It just doesn't grab my attention or stand out like it should.

> Okay, let's talk about some ways we could emphasize different parts of the design.

"SMART" goal planning

SMART goal setting can be a good tool for planning. By incorporating the principles of Specific, Measurable, Actionable, Realistic, and Time-bound goals, you can enhance your strategic planning and improve project management.

Specific. Setting specific goals can help clarify intentions and focus your efforts. You can align resources and support accordingly by clearly defining what you need to accomplish, such as developing a new brand identity or launching a website redesign.

Measurable. You can track progress and evaluate success by establishing measurable goals. Metrics such as client satisfaction ratings, revenue growth, or project completion timelines allow for objective assessment and can help you make informed decisions to optimize performance.

Actionable. SMART goals are intended to be actionable—they outline clear steps and the actions required to achieve them. This approach promotes a proactive mindset within the studio, ensuring that the necessary tasks and milestones are identified and pursued purposefully.

Realistic. Realistic goals take into account available resources, capabilities, and constraints. By setting attainable objectives, you can maintain motivation and prevent frustration. Realistic goals promote a sense of accomplishment, leading to a positive work environment and increased productivity.

Time-bound. Incorporating a time-bound aspect to goals establishes deadlines and creates a sense of urgency. Setting specific timeframes for each objective allows you to stay on track, prioritize tasks, and allocate resources efficiently. This ensures that projects are completed within the desired timeframes, enhancing client satisfaction and fostering a reputation for reliability.

SMART GOAL PLANNER

SPECIFIC	MEASURABLE	ACTIONABLE	REALISTIC	TIME-BOUND

Project management

Another critical part of experiential design education is developing the knowledge and skills to manage projects effectively from start to finish. As we mentioned, during your first client meeting, you will have established the scope of work and due dates for deliverables. Then, you'll need to break the project into bite-sized chunks and assign internal deadlines. For example, DesignWorks at MCAD articulated a project process and lead time estimate based on project type (see *MCAD's DesignWorks process* and *Project lead time* on the following spread). While it might take your team some trial and error to figure out production times, try to have a rough estimate ahead of time. Projects are typically most successful when you check in with your client throughout the process. These check-ins ensure you won't spend an entire semester (or year) working on a project only to discover that you pursued a design direction the client hates.

SETTING TIMELINES

When you ask a potential client about their deadline, try to get an actual date (e.g., "by the end of March"). There are countless times we've heard clients say, "I needed this yesterday" or "I need this ASAP." But when we finally elicit a specific date from them, it turns out they can wait two or three months. Our advice is to give your client a realistic deadline that works with your schedule and within the confines of the class/studio structure. The timeline will work for them or it won't. But by clearly communicating, you can at least be on the same page with a reasonable timeline.

You'll also need to consider the confines of an academic schedule. If you only have your team in a class for a few months, make sure that the project timeline maps onto the course duration. If you have a fully established studio, you might be able to take on longer-term projects. But you still need to ensure that any critical deadlines align with the school year. You don't want to commit to submitting deliverables a week after graduation or in the middle of a holiday break when no one is around to complete the work.

Finally, if a timeframe doesn't work for you, saying no to the project is okay. Coordinating teams can be time-consuming, and you have to worry about other jobs and classes and you need to budget time accordingly. While you might be able to knock out a small design project in a couple of weeks, will your other client projects suffer? Will you ignore your responsibilities for other classes or lose hours and hours of sleep? While a big push once in a while is okay, this can't be the status quo, or it will lead to burnout.

BEGINNING THE WORK

Teams often begin by researching the company or organization, industry, and competitors. A good next step is to produce a few mood boards (with example images, type, and color studies) to help articulate the design direction to a client. You can then ask the client to approve a particular design direction before moving to the next phase. But remember that to get any approvals, you have to know who is making the final decisions. If you're working with a large company, you might interact with many people. Knowing who will be making the final decision will save you a lot of time. Ideally, that person will be present for any meetings or presentations.

Some clients will ask that you send designs in advance of a meeting. If possible, avoid doing this. Your design isn't just about the aesthetic development but also your research and your thought process. You want to be able to share your full scope of work. In addition, these client meetings are a great opportunity to gain experience professionally presenting your designs. Even if a client doesn't approve your design direction, you will have a chance to ask questions.

FIGURE 8.1

MCAD's
DesignWorks
process

MCAD'S DESIGNWORKS PROCESS

Submit intake: Client provides all pertinent information regarding their project (team info, project description, copy and any media assets, delivery dates, etc.).

Project kick-off: Meet with client shortly after intake is submitted. This provides the opportunity to gain more information about the project and discuss key delivery dates.

Comprehensive review: Arrange a comprehensive review of design options. Client is presented with multiple design options in a semi-complete state. Client provides detailed feedback and narrows options.

Proofing: Client reviews physical printouts (at full scale whenever possible) of final designs. Client marks up the printout and/or provides comments. This phase continues until there are no more corrections and the approval form is signed.

Production: The studio oversees production of all projects unless discussed otherwise. This may include simply preparing and sharing web files, or sending projects to print at an offsite facility. Will share printer quotes before sending files to offsite facilities.

Delivery: The studio coordinates delivery of all projects and can also assist with direct mail services.

Wrap-up: If needed, studio will arrange a wrap meeting to review how the process went and discuss any adjustments needed for future projects.

DESIGN WORKS, MCAD

Project lead time

Below are example lead times for DesignWorks, an agency comprised of part-time student designers at the Minneapolis College of Art and Design. Generally the student designers complete over 300 projects every year, while still balancing school and life.

Project type	Lead time needed for intakes
Large catalog	5 months
Small catalog	3.25 months
Campaign/event packet	4 months
Brochure	3 months
Postcard or card	2 months
Title wall	3 months
Identity system	3 months
Poster	2 months
Email	1 month
Advertisement	1.5 months
Signage (outside vendors)	2 months
Tote bags or shirts	2.5 months

Scheduling and coordination

Scheduling and coordination involve a lot of variables, including:
- weekly meetings/office hours
- check-ins/pre-client meetings
- design methods
- internal work flow
- saving work
- documenting final pieces.

It takes attention, intention, and experience to get a feel for how long these steps will take. You may have a limited amount of experience with time and project management, so setting a structure for your group is a huge help. Software or apps can help ease some of this project management. You can also use a simple spreadsheet or whiteboard calendar posted in your workspace. The important thing is that the schedule is always visible to everyone on the team, and you can always refer to it to check on the status of your work.

We recommend adding client meetings and critical deadlines to your calendar first and then breaking those tasks down into their component parts. Assign a student to each task based on their role. Weekly check-ins are also tremendously helpful. You could choose to have a weekly staff meeting, at the start of class, where each team gives a status report. This check-in serves as an accountability check and an opportunity to collectively troubleshoot any issues teams are facing. Each smaller team could then meet and set their targets for the week.

The most important thing to remember: if you won't meet a deadline, clearly communicate this as soon as possible. Then reschedule.

Time management

Whether or not you charge fees, keeping track of time spent on client work will instill good habits and allow you to see how you spend your time. We often under- or over-estimate the time we work on projects (especially when distracted by the internet or social media), so using other tracking methods helps build knowledge about your work habits. There are many software options to help you do this. Apps like *Timeclock* or *TSheets* by Intuit are helpful for logging hours that will eventually lead to invoices and payments. *Toggl* is another free and easy-to-use app that works like a stopwatch to keep track of client jobs. But a good old-fashioned spreadsheet can do the job just as well. Whatever you choose, try to be consistent.

Design Sprint methodology

PHASE 1: UNDERSTAND
Create a shared knowledge base across all participants

PHASE 2: DEFINE
Team evaluates everything they learned in the Understand phase to establish focus

PHASE 3: SKETCH
Generate and share a broad range of ideas as individuals

PHASE 4: DECIDE
Finalize the direction or concept to be prototyped

PHASE 5: PROTOTYPE
Work together to create a prototype of your concept

PHASE 6: VALIDATE
Put your concept in front of users

Google will often implement a week-long "Design Sprint" methodology. If you have an uninterrupted week, this methodology can be beneficial. But even if you don't, you might end up following a similar design research path.

Source: designsprintkit.withgoogle.com/methodology

Conclusion

Forming good relationships can take time. Building a foundation of trust will go a long way. You can develop this with clear communication and delivering your promises consistently and on time.

But remember that trust goes both ways. As much as you might be working hard to find and keep clients, not every client is a good one.

Ideally, the project experience will foster meaningful relationships between students and clients, and your institution will grow industry connections. But sometimes things don't go as planned. The next chapter will explore how (and when) to say "no" to a client, including several ethical considerations for reflection. In addition, we talk about how to find and keep the clients you want (and how to gently get rid of the ones you don't want).

Chapter 8 key concepts

creative brief: a document that outlines the goals and background of a project

intake: the process of starting to work with a client, establishing the scope of work, and determining timelines

lead time: how much time it will take to complete a project

milestone: specific moment in the arc of a project that indicates if you are staying on track with the planned schedule

scope of work: the specifics of the project in terms of quantity

Resources

1. Monteiro, Mike. 2014. *You're My Favorite Client.* New York: A Book Apart.
2. Nelson, Harold G., and Erik Stolterman. 2012. *The Design Way: Intentional Change in an Unpredictable World.* Second edition. Cambridge, Massachusetts; London, England: The MIT Press.

HARD AT WORK

Virginia Tech students working to develop client designs at the DesignUP design marathon.

Chapter 9

Sustaining relationships

Once you've established a good working relationship with a client or community partner and have developed an effective project management system, you must employ strategies to sustain the relationship. These include taking responsibility for the work and paying attention to details. In addition, you may need to weigh up whether or not you'll take on certain kinds of client requests or projects. And if push comes to shove, how do you say "no" to a client? All of these issues come up when you're trying to sustain client relationships that benefit your learning and the client's goals. When all goes well, you might even be able to develop long-term client relationships that last beyond a single term or academic year.

This chapter provides different models for how studios can explore tangible strategies to fit into the structure of any institution. After establishing a track record of positive experiences with clients and community partners, you have the evidence you need to reflect on the value of classroom experiences and how to articulate the value (both monetarily and educationally) to stakeholders.

HOW?

WHO?

WHAT?

WHY?

Attention to detail

Paying attention to detail is one of the most important things to learn when working with design clients and partners. It's a continual process that takes diligence and thoughtfulness. Creating project management tools like checklists and workflows can help guide this work, and it also helps to build steps for others to double-check your work. It's essential that you:

- proofread
- check emails
- check print files/resolution/ do test prints
- check digital files

You also want to think about what might happen, not just what's in front of you at the moment. Can you anticipate anything going wrong in a production process or an event you're planning? Clients will always appreciate it when the designer is proactive and seeks solutions to problems they haven't considered.

> *When we sit in client meetings, I let students take the reins. When I see it's not going the right way, I jump in and hope they see how I'm convincing the clients, hoping they will model my behavior in the future.*
>
> *Gaining client confidence is really important ... I'm willing to let students fail a little bit. They don't have to produce perfect work every time.*
>
> —Marilyn Jones, Professor Emeritus, Lehigh University, Department of Art, Architecture and Design

Ethical considerations for client requests

We touched briefly on ethical considerations in *Chapter 4: Engaging with communities*, and hopefully, your class has established some group values. Here, we focus more on ethical reflections for specific client relationships and projects. We offer this series of questions that can guide you through moments when you're unsure you want to work for a particular client or on a particular project.

What service or product is your client promoting?
Would you still want to take on a client project if it promoted something you don't morally support? For example, would you create an ad campaign promoting e-cigarettes to young audiences? What about one for sugary cereal? Personally, you might or might not care about these sorts of things, but it's worth discussing what type of work you want to produce and what you would not want to do.

Who is your client?
Do your values align with those of your client? For example, would you create a website for a political candidate with a track record of gerrymandering? Would you design a logo for a bakery that refused service to LGBTQ+ patrons? Many companies specialize in numerous fields which can create a bit of a gray zone. You might be asked to develop design services for one sub-brand while the parent company is also a part of the big tobacco industry. Would you still want to partner with that client? What if that client could pay triple your typical rate?

How is the design going to be implemented?
What is your client asking you to create? Does your client want you to design single-use mass-produced objects when other options are available? Would they be open to a discussion about more sustainable solutions? Where will the product be produced and are employees there offered a fair wage? Could you encourage the client to go with a local manufacturer?

Notice that we asked a lot of questions and didn't give a whole lot of answers. It would help if you reflect on what you care most about. Where do you draw the line in the sand? Also, you might not be in a financial position to be overly picky about your clients. Regardless, we encourage you to pause from time to time to think about such practices and to help steer your clients toward more ethical and sustainable solutions.

When to say "no"

You learn as much—or more—from bad experiences as you do from good ones. So, as much as we'd like all of our client experiences and collaborations to be a success, you might even learn more from the worst ones. Another challenge to managing client relationships is establishing healthy boundaries. Some clients might email too often, or call you regularly after hours and on weekends. Or they might ask for round after round of revisions, even though you have gone way past your agreed-upon scope of work. Often, you can practice some "small no's" in these instances. You could post an out-of-office email response from Friday at 5pm until Monday at 9am. Or if a client asks you to do extra design work, tell them you will gladly create a new estimate for the additional work.

Unfortunately, sometimes a client relationship cannot be salvaged. It's usually pretty clear when you reach this point, but that doesn't mean it's easy to sever ties.

Generally, there are a few reasons why you might want to fire a client.
1. They do not treat students with respect or care about their learning.
2. You can't produce the work they want in the timeframe they need. Hopefully, this can be established before you begin working together, but sometimes you'll discover that it's a bad client/designer fit and is best to part ways.
3. Too many people are making decisions which often leads to contradictory feedback and indecision.
4. The client breaks ethical boundaries (e.g., one advisor told us how they found out a client had hired multiple agencies at the same time!) and isn't willing to pivot.

If a client relationship isn't going well, you'll want to involve your faculty advisor immediately. These kinds of interactions are difficult for even the most seasoned designers, and it helps to develop a unified strategy together to support you and your team members.

JULIETTE CEZZAR

Ultimately, a project is worth taking if:

1. you will make something you love,
2. the money is good,
3. the experience of working on the project is enjoyable or fulfilling, or
4. some combination of the above.

—The AIGA Guide to Careers in Graphic & Communication Design

Articulating value

Throughout this book, we articulate the value of client-based experiences and student-run studios. They are an opportunity for student empowerment, give you real-world experience while still in the safety of a classroom, and build bridges to a broader community. But if you're trying to articulate the value of your particular club, class, or studio, it's worth reflecting on what you hope to (or currently) get out of such experiences. We recommend a brainstorming session. Here are a few questions to get you started:

If you have not yet started taking on client work, consider:
- Why do you want to have client experiences?
- Where do you want to integrate the client work (e.g., in a class, as a club, as a dedicated studio)?
- How would the client work enhance the existing curriculum?
- What would you select as your areas of specialization?

If you already have experience with client work in the classroom, consider:
- What have you gained from the client work so far?
- What could be done to improve the interactions?
- What is your ideal scope of work?
- What are your needs?

Support from stakeholders

To sustain client-based work in the design classroom, you need support and buy-in from all key stakeholders, including students, faculty, administration, clients, and community partners.

STUDENTS

First and foremost, do you and your classmates want to be working with clients? Are you willing to dedicate a few hours each week to gain real-world experience? Would you be interested in taking a class dedicated to client work? Would you be willing to serve in a leadership capacity? If you gave a resounding "yes" to any or all of these questions, it's worth trying to get buy-in from faculty, administrators, clients, and community partners.

FACULTY

The heaviest burden of managing client work in the classroom falls on faculty. To have successful experiences, they must dedicate a tremendous amount of their time, often as an overload on their normal teaching, service, and research responsibilities. If you're looking to launch a fully-fledged design studio, you'll want the support of most of the faculty—even if only one faculty is fully dedicated to the studio management. This buy-in is essential, as a studio will require resources (like space, equipment, and faculty time)—and many departments are already struggling to get what they need.

It's also important to garner broader support to ensure the studio isn't overly dependent on one faculty member. What happens if that person gets sick, has a baby, or takes another job? Does the studio just close its doors? Additional faculty members can also share their expertise or give critiques on occasion.

If you're wondering how you might convince faculty or administrators, remember that client work in the classroom is a tremendous benefit for students and can be a way to distinguish your program from others. As someone who ran a studio for years, Meaghan often serves as a reference for former students. She often hears employers say, "This experience sets your students apart from the other applicants I spoke with. They had experience working with clients and applied projects that others weren't getting until months or years of working after graduation."

ADMINISTRATORS
If student success isn't enough to convince administrators to allocate resources, you could also imagine and develop the future vision together. What would you want it to look like if you were to develop a student-run course or studio? **How could it enhance your existing curriculum?** If you have a physical studio, could this visually be a selling point for your school? Many design studios look cool. Students could design large-scale graphics to capture the attention of visitors. Then, when you're giving prospective students tours of your facilities, you have something fun and exciting to show them.

Additionally, many design programs are relatively low-budget compared to some peer programs. For example, many studio art programs require large painting or sculpture spaces and individual studios for students. Many industrial design and architecture programs have expensive fabrication labs. **If your program draws in many students but doesn't yet have equivalent resources for your students, why not?** Additionally, a student-run studio could be a school-wide venture where you work with other disciplines—such as creative technologies, video artists, or entrepreneurship—to give all students these valuable real-world experiences.

CLIENT OR COMMUNITY PARTNERS
One way to quickly form a studio is to find a big client or partner to fund the establishment. If you have an extensive client project or donation, you might be able to cover equipment, salaries, and more. But once you start to get in "big money" situations, you'll want to ensure you're working with your supervisor and possibly your institution's fiscal manager or advancement staff. You'll likely need contracts to protect yourself.

You might have the opportunity to work on a huge client project and be paid handsomely for it, but do you have the faculty and students available to do the work? Even if the answer is "no," you might be able to if you can plan ahead. If you have a lead time of six months or a year, you might be able to hire a graduate student or adjunct professor to assist with work. You would also have time to get students to commit, possibly even running a special topics course dedicated to the client project. But if you don't have the bandwidth to complete the requested work in the necessary timeframe, it is okay to say "no."

Conclusion

Many educators develop client partnerships that become ongoing and evolve into long-term relationships over several years. In these scenarios, students see how goals and projects evolve, especially when each project is well documented so that future students can reference past work. In this chapter, we described how ethical considerations arise in client relationships and the questions you can ask to assess your willingness to do the work. Sometimes, this requires you to decide whether or not you'll say "no" to a potential project. In the end, reflections and interactions like these help you articulate the value of your client work to gain support from stakeholders—students, faculty, administrators, and client and community partners. With everyone on board, amazing experiences will take shape.

Chapter 9 key concept

stakeholder: a person or organization with an interest in a project; the outcome matters to them, so their input is sought and valued

Part four

How?

CHAPTER 10

Launching a studio

CHAPTER 11

Managing the money

CHAPTER 12

Planning for the future

TAKING IT TO THE NEXT LEVEL

Students critique work in Sarah Rutherford's Corporate Identity class at Cleveland State University.

Space: finding your home

If you're lucky enough to have some say in the matter, you can decide if you want to be physically located on your institution's campus, or if you would rather be off-campus. While it is convenient to have a studio near other classes and faculty, there are some benefits to being embedded in the community. For instance, if you can have a "storefront" presence, you'll have greater visibility, which can be one way to get new clients. You might also be seen as being more a part of the community. Additionally, by moving off-campus, you wouldn't be taking any existing facilities away.

What happens if you don't have a home? Perhaps you have no operating budget, and every square inch of space is already in use. If that's the case, it's okay to start small. Maybe your group operates more like a "club" and meets after class hours in your classroom space. Or, if you're part of a larger institution, get creative about space. Ask if there's a conference room or a space in a general-use facility. You might even get a standing weekly reservation of a room so your group could have a consistent meeting place, which will come in handy when you have client meetings.

If space is an issue, you can also go to your clients. Ask if you can meet them at their company, or in a space in their community, such as a coffee house or place of significance to the project. Even if you have a dedicated facility, observing clients and community partners in their own home base will give you greater insight, and can sometimes put the client at greater ease.

SPACE TO WORK

FourDesign students at work in their dedicated conference room.

INTERVIEW: *Maria Rogal, Mint Design Studio, University of Florida*

Maria Rogal, MFA, is a Professor in the School of Art & Art History at the University of Florida. She is also Affiliate Faculty in the Center for Latin American Studies and the Center for Arts, Migration, and Entrepreneurship. Her research interests include co-design, design with the pluriverse, and equitable design. Much of her design work and research is based in México. She is a faculty advisor of Mint Design Studio, a faculty-supervised, student-run graphic design studio that was established in 2002 with the goal of providing advanced design students the opportunity to apply design in real-world contexts.

Can you describe your program's client-based experience?
It's been an evolution. We're going on 21 years of a client-based experience. Currently, we operate as a required course to provide graphic design majors experience working with clients, with what we call a "safety net." This course is relatively small because it requires the agility of the instructor and a lot of hands-on work to coordinate with the students. Even though we have a framework for projects, every project is different.

We want to augment the design opportunities that people have to work with designers in the community. We are in a university town, and there are many designers here doing great work. We don't want to take away from their work, but we're looking at work that might have a little bit longer time scale. We charge what we think is 10% of a professional practice fee. So we're not undercutting anybody, and we want that to be clear.

Could you describe the course learning outcomes?
The main outcome is to provide students with opportunities to work collaboratively and in different roles. Some students might be project leads, but everybody's a designer and working together. We want them to learn how to apply design in a real-world context where they understand that it is not what they and the others in their classroom studios might want to do, but what the real needs of the client/partner are.

How do you initially make contact with your clients?
One of the challenges to doing that is maintaining stability and visibility within the community. We do this through building networks of people who are interested in education and by identifying organizations that will benefit from design and who are going to be reciprocal and relational.

How do you think about equitable practices when engaging students with these external partners and clients?

We often begin by discussing what we want to get out of the course and framing it in terms of respectful interactions. It's a really great chance to educate people about stepping into other communities. An equitable practice is to use our expertise but not think that we are the only experts in the room.

We also talk about ethical issues and how we do not want to parachute in, do something, and leave. We're looking to build long-term relationships. We're also looking to build design knowledge and different ways of working within communities that might be different from professional design practice. We reflect on where our interests lie and what our values are.

We call "going out of the studio into communities" design fieldwork, where we are observing spaces, looking at the details, looking at the bigger picture. We do research. For example, the 1619 series of articles has been particularly influential in understanding systemic issues in the United States, and many other resources are important. We bring in reading about pluriversality, but we also make sure that we are not—as much as we can—not creating spaces where students themselves or partners feel othered. That's been critical for us.

What are the biggest challenges for students in this kind of experience?

Understanding the value of doing this work in an educational environment that may not be as quick or as directed or as deliverable-oriented as a four-week classroom project. Grasping the soft skills that you are learning and what they are and the value of those, particularly when things don't go as planned or according to the timeline—and that it doesn't mean that anybody did anything wrong. We frame recalibrating and refiguring as a positive thing. How to be flexible, how to be resilient, how to pivot, and how to push a project just a little bit further.

What do you think are the biggest rewards of this kind of experience?

Having experiences outside of the classroom that cause you to have to think critically and creatively about what you are doing as a designer. How do you start to talk about your work, how do you frame your work, how do you unpack it for people so they can understand some of the thought process that goes into designing and that it's not only a fun thing sitting in the corner—but there's also a lot of research, collaboration, and process that goes into it. To really foster that designer mindset where you understand that the world is changing, but you are flexible enough and resilient enough to work in it and with people as we change in order to create the kind of world that we want.

Is there any additional advice that you might give a student participating in this kind of program?

I think the most important thing is to be open and to be curious and to trust the process and to trust the people that you are working with. Being open also means communicating any discomfort you might have or questions you might have or challenges or problems you might see. This is not about winning, but it's about working together. It's really about design collectives, which we see so much in practice and also so many things coming out as designers wanting to work cooperatively. This is a collaborative field. The more that we can learn how to do this in school with a safety net and build those relationships, the better. ■

Conclusion

As we've discussed, there are many things to research, analyze, and decide when launching a student-run design studio. But it's worth the time to plan and assess before jumping right into action. Mike Goldberg at Bentley speaks about preparing a detailed contingency plan before launching client-based work, especially in a more formal structure like a studio. The more you look and act like a business, the more you must respond like one. For example, what happens if a project starts to go awry? Or there's a problem with a student? What's your plan B and plan C?

Aligning your values to a possible market position will help you develop a value proposition, identify what you need to really get things going, and develop contingency plans. Then you're launched! After things get going, most studios don't struggle to get clients, and many have a waiting list. So the next chapter explores the question we get asked the most—how do you manage the money (or not) of doing client work in a student-run studio?

Chapter 10 key concepts

market position: how customers see or think about a particular company or brand

SWOT analysis: an exercise for analysing strengths, weaknesses, opportunities, and threats of a business, organization, or idea

value proposition: the unique offering that a company, product, or service provides to a customer

References

1. "Design Futures Research | AIGA." n.d. AIGA. aiga.org/resources/design-futures-research.
2. Hannam, Ben. 2013. *A Graphic Design Student's Guide to Freelance: Practice Makes Perfect*. Hoboken, NJ: John Wiley & Sons.

MAKING CONNECTIONS

Student from NC State College of Design working with Red Hat on a sponsored research project.

Chapter 11

Managing the money

One of the biggest challenges of running a studio is keeping on top of financial operations, such as tracking your budget and expenses, writing contracts, and billing. Try to develop a sustainable model and make annual adjustments. Even if your studio doesn't charge clients, or works exclusively with not-for-profits, you will have expenses—or, at the very least, things you need to purchase, such as printing supplies or equipment.

This chapter will explore various financial models in detail, including how those models operate within a larger institution. You'll need to consider how to market the studio and manage financial operations, including budgets, expenses, contracts, and invoices. We will also describe the sponsorship model and alternative financial options.

HOW? WHO? WHAT? WHY?

Developing a strategic plan and budget

In the dream scenario, you have a huge chunk of change and can go wild buying the latest and greatest furniture—maybe even a cool Eames lounge chair or two! That said, even if you have a luxurious startup fund, you'll want to first plan out ALL of your expenses by dividing them into startup (one-time) expenses and ongoing (recurring) expenses. You might also consider some of your costs that could arise irregularly or periodically every few years. Salaries could also be an expense. Some studios generate enough revenue to pay a partial salary, such as an assistant salary, graduate student stipend, and/or student wages. See *Budget considerations* on the next page for fairly common example expenses. Of course, you might have fewer or more expenses than those listed.

> *Design Lab continues to be one of my most rewarding experiences in my time in teaching. I get to see students grow in their skills and confidence and become young professionals. I get to see the veteran students mentor the rookies. I get to see clients who are amazed by the professionalism, knowledge, and skills of the students.*
>
> —Wade Lough, Associate Professor of Graphic Design, Longwood University

BUDGET CONSIDERATIONS

Example expenses

Try to plan for a few years in advance, or at the very least, a year ahead. If you ask for start-up costs, plan beyond the next semester or two. Remember that many costs will be ongoing. For instance, if you have a computer lab, you might have to pay for software subscriptions each month for each machine. If you have a physical space, you might need to sign contracts lasting for several years.

Example start-up expenses
- Equipment
  - Computers
  - Tablets
  - Phones
  - Scanners
  - Printers
  - Cameras/video equipment
- Furniture
  - Desks
  - Chairs
  - Conference table
  - Lounge furniture
- Signage
- Website development
- Space deposit

Salaries
- Faculty salary (or partial)
- Student wages/stipend
- Graduate assistantship
- Fiscal/business manager
- IT/technician funding

Example monthly expenses
- Subscriptions
  - Software
  - Internet
  - Phone bill
  - Printer expenses
  - Domain and web hosting
  - Magazine subscriptions
  - Server/online storage
- Rent

Irregular expenses
- Fonts
- Stock photography/illustrations/video
- Advertising
- Design competition entry fees
- Design books/educational materials
- Printing promotional materials
- Travel

Periodic (every few years) expenses
- New furniture
- New computers/printers/scanners

Even if you're operating as a nonprofit and your goal is to zero out (where your profits match your expenses) at the end of each fiscal year, you often have the ability to save for some equipment and longer-term funding. A studio rarely makes enough in one year to buy a whole new lab's worth of furniture or computers, but large purchases are more feasible when averaged out over several years.

Fiscal support

Does your institution have a fiscal or business manager? If so, ask for their help. Not only can they assist you in establishing your budget and a fund through your institution, but they might think of a few things that you didn't. For example, suppose you are paying students or covering a portion of staff/faculty salaries. In that case, some institutions require that you also contribute to "salary overhead," which might be an extra 5-20% cost. If you do not have a fiscal manager, you'll still want to make sure you're communicating with any supervisors. Institutions seem to care a LOT as soon as money is involved. You might also consider hiring a Certified Public Accountant (CPA) or a lawyer to help establish your organization. Whatever your situation, consider the following questions:

- Do you need a business license, or do you need to establish yourself as a "center" at your institution?
- Do you need to start a checking account or create a fund through your department?
- Are you established as a not-for-profit (which in many countries can give you a tax break) or a for-profit organization?
- And if you're operating as a for-profit, **do NOT forget to save money for taxes!**

To charge or not to charge?

Not all client work is paid. Additionally, money isn't the only contribution clients can give to student groups. They can provide goods and services—anything from buying design books for students to giving vouchers for their products (e.g., if you design work for a restaurant, they could give students gift cards). In one of Meaghan's design classes, they did some unpaid work for a river float company, and the client gave all the students free passes to go tubing. **Sometimes, the benefit of partnerships isn't financial.** Perhaps you're getting to contribute to a group that does good work for your community, such as a public garden, a food bank, or a library that offers free educational programs.

But broadly speaking, you'll probably decide to either charge for work or not.

While getting paid sounds great, it also adds a significant amount to your workload, especially for the initial establishment. You'll need to ensure you are equipped and able to accept funds.

Some smaller studios and student groups work around the time-intensive logistics of accepting monetary payment by accepting "donations" instead. These funds often have fewer restrictions on how they can be spent, but there are limits to this system. If a client project takes longer than expected, you cannot bill for overtime. In addition, you would usually bill a client 25% to 50% upfront and bill the remainder upon completion (although some choose to bill monthly or semi-annually, particularly for larger projects). When working with this model, if a client decides not to pay, you cannot force someone to donate.

ADVANTAGES AND DISADVANTAGES BY TYPE OF FINANCIAL STRUCTURE

	EXTERNAL CLIENTS	INTERNAL CLIENTS	COMMUNITY PARTNERS	COMBINATION
MONETARY/ FOR-PROFIT	Pro: Can be a financial benefit Pro: Students have the opportunity to work with a wide array of clients Con: Taxes and how these organizations relate to parent companies can be a challenge Con: Must handle billing external entities that are often difficult Con: Might be seen as competition with local design agencies	Pro: Can build recognition Pro: Develops relationships with organizations and learns about other areas of specialization Con: If a client project does not go well, it can be awkward so close to home Con: Might require regular financial reviews	Pro: Might be able to work with one or two larger companies on larger-scale research Pro: Often community partners can have large-scale budgets Con: If a large community partnership does not work out, you might not have a good project for that term	Pro: Lots of flexibility in work Con: Difficult to plan what each term will look like
NONPROFIT	Similar to "for-profit" set-up, except profits and expenses will need to annually balance one another out.			
NON-MONETARY	Pro: Students still have the chance to gain "real world" experience Con: Clients have less accountability when you aren't charging because they have no financial stake in the game	Pro: Your program can be viewed as a benefit to the overall institution Con: The role of design is sometimes viewed as a "service" and less of a "partnership"	Pro: You can positively contribute to the community Con: You might feel like companies or community partners aren't paying for services when they could possibly afford to	Pro: Without worrying about charging, you can take on work that aligns with your values Con: You will still have studio expenses and without a source of income, you have to absorb these costs

Compensating students

Depending on the profitability of your studio, you might be able to compensate students. If students are paid, check with your institution to see what regulations are in place. You may need to use a time-keeping system and pay employees based on an established hourly wage. Some schools allow lump sums to be paid, while others require hourly logs. We know of studios that pay different rates (e.g., an Art Director is paid a higher hourly rate than a Junior Designer), or only pay certain positions. Other studios pay everyone the same rate.

While the most straightforward option is to pay students, this isn't the only option. If your studio doesn't have enough funding to pay students, or if you'd rather be investing in other areas, you can compensate students in other ways:
- Scholarships
- Design supplies (e.g., books, sketchbooks, equipment)
- Access to equipment
  (e.g., 24/7 studio access with photo equipment and computer lab)
- Free printing or hosting
- Fun swag (e.g., branded shirts, patches, buttons, water bottles, bags, stickers)
- Trips (e.g., studio visits, annual trip to a city)
- Internship credit/class credit

SWAG

Some of the goodies given to participants of the DesignUP design marathon as a thank you for volunteering

Choosing client partnerships

In deciding whether to charge for your work, you'll also consider what kind of clients you want to work with. Clients can be internal (from another part of your organization) or external (a business or organization outside your institution).

Many large universities have enough need for design services that a studio could be busy full-time just by creating departmental websites, promotions, and presentations. Getting paid for internal work is often as simple as getting a transfer of funding from another department to your own. It's also quite easy to meet face-to-face with clients when you only have to walk across campus. However, one downside to working solely with internal clients is the work can be redundant. You might get tired of using the same two Pantone colors and the official university typefaces required by their brand standards. In addition, even if client relationships deteriorate, you still have to work with the client as long as you're with the institution.

External partnerships can take shape as a paid client or reciprocal work. If you're primarily interested in doing good and giving back to your community, considering the pedagogical value of partnering with nonprofits and community partners. These relationships can be incredibly meaningful, and you might even develop long-term partnerships in which you build upon work each year. But as we know, running a studio isn't free, so you might not have the luxury of unpaid work. Or perhaps you can only afford to take on one unpaid project per term. In addition, it's a great experience to get to work with paying clients, and it can also be fun. (Even when it's not, you can still learn a lot!) However, **getting external clients to pay the bill sometimes resembles herding cats, so you'll want to make sure you have explicitly defined expectations and a written agreement before you begin work.**

FIELD WORK

Students from Mint Design Studio, University of Florida, doing field work.

Estimates, contracts, and invoices—*oh my!*

Every project should have documentation that clearly communicates the project's goals, including the scope of work, timeline and deadlines, and terms of compensation. Create estimates before the project starts, use contracts to demonstrate agreement from everyone involved, and send invoices once the project is completed (or sometimes part of the way through a project and again at the end).

ESTIMATES

When writing estimates, always include time for revisions. Edits often take as long (or longer) as the original work. Be sure to write a clause for "additional charges" when a client exceeds the agreed-upon number of corrections. Before we ever charge a client more than the estimate, we warn them that we have exceeded the expectations of the original contract. That way, the additional charges never come as a shock to them. Remember to specify what work is covered by a proposal, particularly when working for a flat fee. Otherwise, you could get bogged down with rounds of unpaid revisions. Include the following information on any estimate:

- Date
- Client name and contact information
- Your studio name and contact information
- Scope of work
- Deliverables
- Payment and any pre-payment (e.g., 25% down before start of work)
    - Estimate either your hours and hourly rate or agree a flat fee
    - State how many rounds of revisions are included and what your hourly fee is if the project goes over.

Things to note:
- Get the estimate signed before you begin work.
- Give a copy to the client (ideally by email so you have a record) and keep a copy.
- Do not use the phrase "work for hire" unless you're willing to forfeit your ownership rights to the client.
- You might add a clause that states, "Client agrees to pay the estimate amount and up to 10% higher," or "This is an estimate based on hours, and the final total might be higher or lower."

CONTRACTS

Once the estimate is signed, it serves as your primary work contract. Some clients will request additional work contracts, such as a non-disclosure agreement (NDA). **Since NDAs can cover a wide array of restrictions, read the fine print carefully.** If your institution offers legal services, request a meeting with them to review the contract to understand the parameters fully. NDAs for design work often have restrictions like, "You cannot show any images of this work for X number of years." Before taking on this kind of project, reflect on whether or not it's worth it to your group. If you and your peers cannot use this project in your portfolio (or, in some cases, not even be able to mention what client you worked for), what are the main benefits of working with the client? Alternatively, consider taking on a client that will let you showcase their work.

Intellectual property—designed work that can be copyrighted, patented, or trademarked—is another contract consideration. Many clients or partners in sponsored research will want to retain the intellectual property rights to a project. While you might be okay with a *paying* client or partner retaining intellectual property rights, if you are not being compensated, you'll want to retain the intellectual property rights.

A NOTE ON SPEC WORK:

Spec work (aka speculative work) is design work provided to prospective clients without first establishing a fee for such services in writing. Occasionally, clients will ask designers to give them a direction before agreeing to pay for anything. Sometimes this just requires a little client education, in which you gently but firmly articulate the value of design ideas and explain the process and time that goes into your work. Other times, this client is trying to get something for nothing—not cool!

The most common form of this is design competitions. For example, a company might create a logo design competition rather than hire a designer to create a logo for them. In this sort of competition, many designers do work with no compensation.

WORKING WITH VENDORS

As you write your contract, you will also want to specify whether you will manage (and possibly pay for) printing or web hosting. Sometimes, a client will want to give you a lump sum for a project that covers everything. If you pay for printing and/or hosting out of your pocket, you can charge a markup (usually between 10% and 25%) for these services. This can be a nice way to earn a little extra money, but if something goes wrong with printing, you are on the hook for additional costs. Web hosting expenses are fairly straightforward, but you'll want to confirm you can keep the websites live for years to come. If you end up hosting many sites (and offering website updates) over the years, this can become a full-time job. Other common contracted elements include:

- Photography/illustrations
- Videography
- Copywriting
- Font purchases.

If a project calls for additional materials such as copy and images, you can either request (in writing!) that the client provides them or include them as line items in your contract. If you think you might need to buy some typefaces or stock imagery, include those estimated expenses as well. It's better to charge a client less than the estimate than return to them asking for a bigger budget.

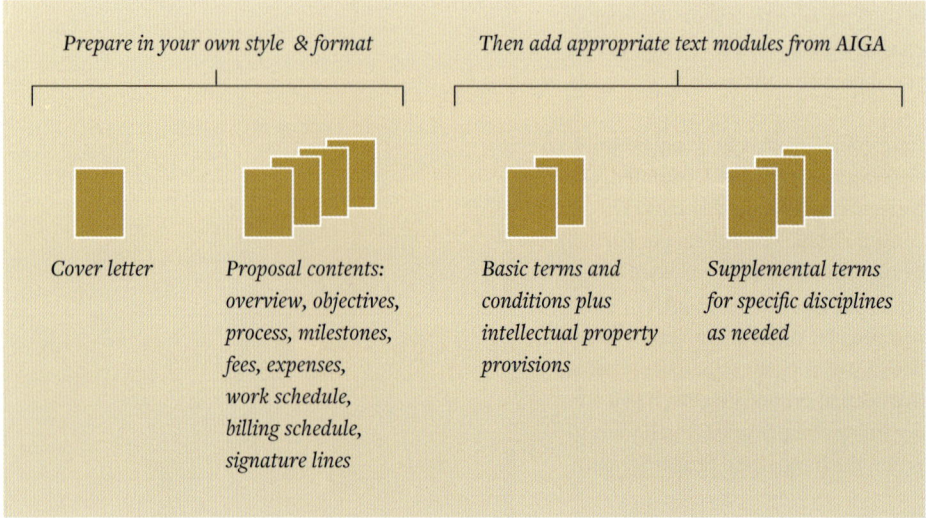

AIGA provides some wonderful resources for freelancers, including example contracts that can be customized: aiga.org/resources/business-freelance-resources They also provided the above diagram.[1]

INVOICES

As soon as your design work is complete, create an invoice. **There should not be any surprises in the invoice.** If you charged a flat fee for a product (e.g., a brochure or a four-page website), your invoice should be very straightforward. If you were charging an hourly rate, show how many hours you spent on the project as well as including the hourly rate. As mentioned earlier, you should communicate with your client if the total will be higher than originally estimated. Most contracts will specify that the final total might be higher than estimated.

The invoice should include:
- the word "invoice"
- date
- client name and contact information
- your studio name and contact
- flat rate OR Hours + hourly rate
- any additional agreed-upon purchases (e.g., fonts, photographs, domain name)
- total amount due
- something to the effect of, "pay within 30 days of receipt."

You might also add a longer clause that states something to the effect of, "If not paid within 30 days, the client will owe an additional 5% of the total."

Send the invoice promptly. If your institution has a business/fiscal manager, you can copy them on the email so they know to follow up and can update their billing. In the body of the email, you can also tell the client that it was a pleasure working with them (if it was!) and share links to any final deliverables if you haven't already done so.

If you do not hear back within 30 days, follow up with a reminder email and re-attach the invoice. Usually, a gentle nudge does the trick. Sometimes, people are just busy and forget! Other times, it takes some pestering. If you've sent two reminders and still haven't heard back, contact your supervisor or legal services to see what they recommend as the next step.

A NOTE ON LICENSING AGREEMENTS

Occasionally, a client will approach you with a less traditional project idea, such as a licensing agreement, in which your group designs products and receives a percentage of each sale. A typical example is designing university goods such as mugs, shirts, wrapping paper, and cards.

If you choose to work on this sort of project, consider the following:
- *Is your entire payment a percentage of sales, or are you paid up-front as well? If you receive any up-front payment, you would likely receive a smaller percentage of sales, but these are both areas that can be negotiated.*
- *How often will you receive payments? Monthly? Quarterly?*
- *How will you receive payments? Directly from the merchant? From the client?*

INTERNALLY FUNDED STUDIO MODEL

Some studios are funded by their institution and do not need to charge clients. Others might receive some supplemental support, so they have a little less financial pressure. Since some studios run as classes, departments will occasionally give tuition profit or class fees back to the group. Other times, institutions have large endowments with capital to spare—but unfortunately, this is a rarity. More commonly, departments look for ways that a studio could help financially, such as paying a portion of faculty/staff salaries or supporting graduate assistantships. In fact, these cost savings could be one of your strongest arguments for gaining administrative support for such a program.

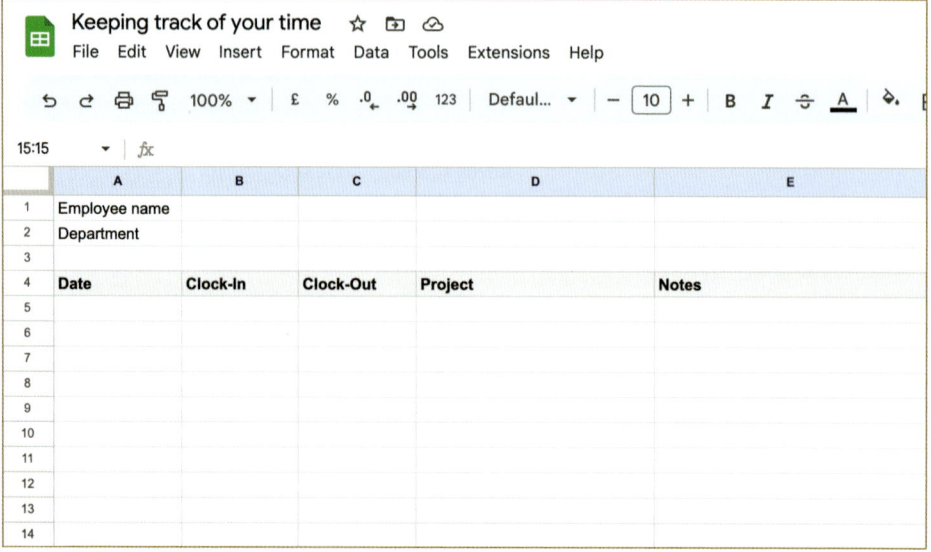

KEEPING TRACK OF YOUR TIME

If you're charging an hourly rate, you must keep track of your time. There are many apps to help you with this, and most will allow you to keep track by project. If that's too complicated, a good old-fashioned spreadsheet will do just fine. For many of you, this might be the first time you've had to keep track of the time you spend designing, and it can be a difficult habit to start. But it won't just help you accurately bill clients, it will also help you estimate how long tasks will take you in the future.

Sponsored research: an alternative to traditional client work

Sponsored research is a project in which a company provides funding to a group in order to conduct research of a specific focus and scope. This can take shape as part of a class or a studio. The funding could cover basic costs (e.g., faculty salary) or beyond (e.g., establishment of a large department research fund). The larger goal of a sponsored studio is the generation of new knowledge.

For example, a company could approach a department and ask students to explore possibilities for integrating a conversational interface into a specific software platform for a blind or mobility-impaired user. Or, perhaps, students could research and prototype an interface that draws from machine learning capabilities in order to respond to individual user needs. More broadly, the project might stem from a newly identified pain point that the company wants to address. In these situations, the project should be something future-facing that the company is interested in exploring, but doesn't have the time to dig into. The students shouldn't be doing the same kind of project that a company's employees regularly undertake, but rather they should work outside the regular workflow in a more speculative research space. Ultimately, the goal is not to produce a patentable project but rather a prototype that inspires possible directions.

This sponsored research content is based on the research of Helen Armstrong (read more at helenarmstrong.info).

SPONSORED STUDIOS	INDUSTRY COLLABORATIONS	INDUSTRY PROJECTS
Future-facing projects, with funding from industry partners, where students work with industry to conduct research and develop prototypes. *NDA, intellectual property (IP) belongs to company (funding).*	*Good for grads and undergrads* *No NDA, intellectual property (IP) belongs to students (no funding).*	*Good for undergrads* *Company shares a design challenge previously completed by their own employees so that students might emulate a real life workflow (no funding). Student work should not take the place of employee efforts.*

CASE STUDY: *Red Hat*

NC STATE—HELEN ARMSTRONG—GRAPHIC DESIGN SPONSORED RESEARCH

Helen Armstrong, Director of the MGXD Program and Professor of Graphic & Experience Design at North Carolina State University, has overseen numerous sponsored studios, primarily focused on UX research and scenario videos that demonstrate the resulting prototype in use. Armstrong and her students have also worked on unfunded industry collaborations, in which students work with companies to conduct research and design interfaces.

CLIENT: Red Hat[2]
COURSE: GD400 (seniors, undergraduate)
PROJECT LENGTH: 9 weeks

Seniors spent nine weeks digging into autonomous vehicles (AV), data collection, and interface design with a team from Red Hat. This project asked students to consider topics like data privacy and security, open data sets, edge computing, and machine learning.

CENTRAL RESEARCH QUESTION:
How might the data collected by an AV benefit human passengers and communities in ways unrelated to the functionality of the car?

For this project, student groups first identified potential communities that might use AVs in the future. These communities ranged from roofers, to carpooling parents, to elderly travelers. The students then worked with Red Hat to gather information and conduct interviews so that they might develop personas (fictional characters that are based on accumulated research to help envision user needs and desires).

CASE STUDY: *Red Hat*

NC STATE—HELEN ARMSTRONG—GRAPHIC DESIGN SPONSORED RESEARCH

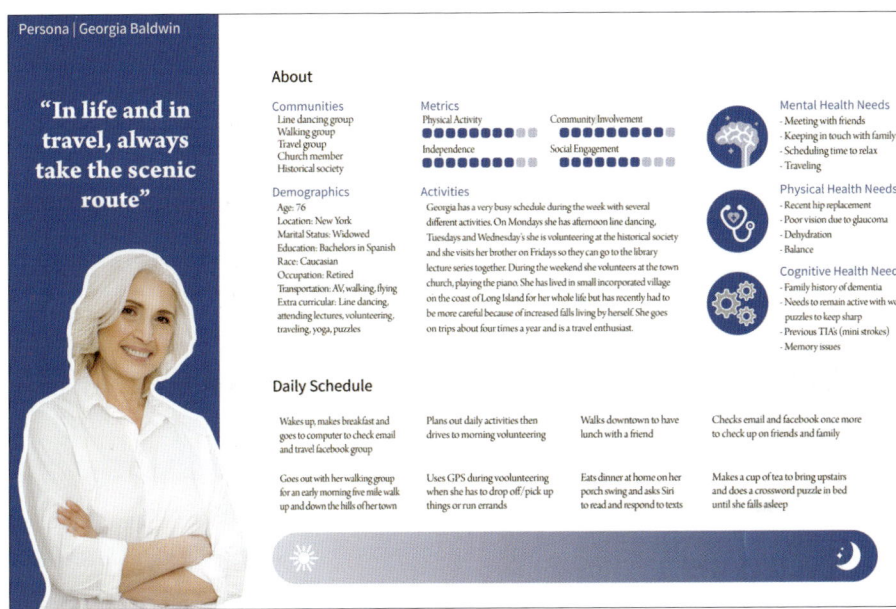

USER JOURNEY MAPS

Based on these interviews and secondary research, students then created journey maps detailing each persona's current daily workflow. These maps help designers pinpoint persona struggles, or pain points, as well as potential innovation points. Students also gathered benchmarking data (a comparative analysis of successful interfaces currently gathering data to benefit communities).

194 CASE STUDY: Red Hat
NC STATE—HELEN ARMSTRONG—GRAPHIC DESIGN SPONSORED RESEARCH

DATA POSSIBILITY MATRIX

Because this project specifically addressed the capabilities of machine learning (ML), students filled out a huge matrix that matched ML capabilities to the pain points and opportunities they had earlier identified. After generating lots of ideas, they began sketching as a part of their iterative ideation process.

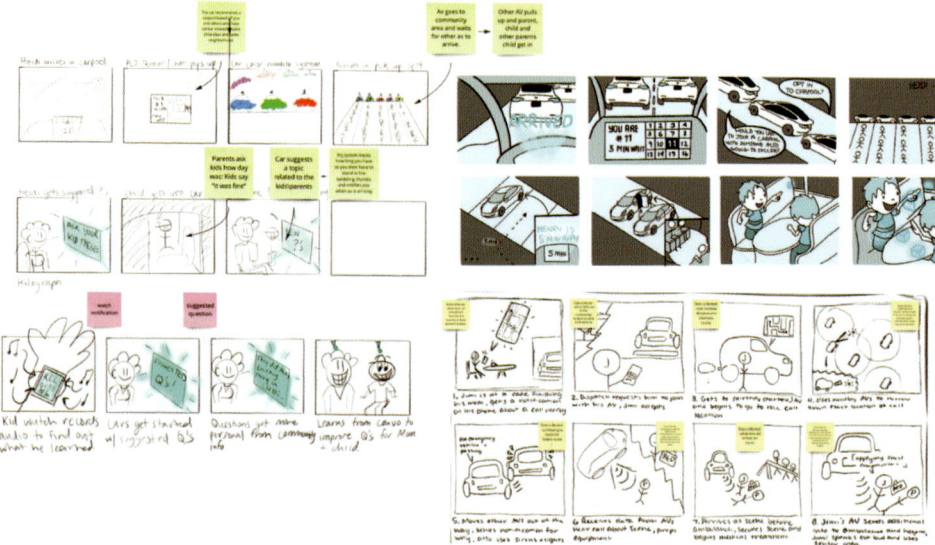

STORYBOARDS

To communicate potential user experiences, students created storyboards, which they shared with Red Hat during critique sessions. Based on the resulting feedback, students continued to refine and to develop their concepts.

CASE STUDY: *Red Hat*
NC STATE—HELEN ARMSTRONG—GRAPHIC DESIGN SPONSORED RESEARCH

UI AND SCENARIO DEVELOPMENT

At the end of this project, each team presented hi-fidelity prototypes of potential AV interfaces, as well as scenario videos that demonstrated personas using the interfaces. Scenario videos force designers to address how the interface might be used throughout an individual's workflow. Red Hat was able to view the videos to gain insight into various potential user groups and make informed decisions around future resource allocation.

GREATEST CHALLENGES

Large research projects like this require a tremendous amount of coordination by the students, the professor, and the company. All participants must be committed to a successful project outcome. In addition, students often struggle to work productively together in teams. The project becomes an opportunity for them to learn collaborative design and strengthen their own interpersonal communication skills.

GREATEST REWARD

Students were able to move through the entire design process, from initial research and problem formation, to a flushed out interface and user experience. Working with a company like Red Hat enabled the students to interact with a range of experts (developers, UX designers, engineers, transportation consultants) that are not accessible in a typical classroom project. In addition, the students were able to share their finished work directly with top level executives rather than slowly working their way up through a company.

Marketing your agency

We touched on marketing in *Chapter 8*, but we want to make sure you consider your overall marketing strategy as it ties into your overall budget—even if, and especially if, you're working on a shoestring budget. While you do not directly profit from documenting your work and self-promotion, these are the most prominent ways you'll likely attract new clients. Once you have a project or two under your belt, share documentation. Remember to take photos and save process work along the way so you aren't scrambling to find imagery later on. When sharing projects publicly, take the time to color-correct and edit your images and present your design solutions in the best possible light. If you can, get photos of your design work. If that isn't possible, create customized and professional mock-ups. Write compelling descriptions and proofread your text.

Here are a few marketing considerations with their potential expenses:
- **Advertisements:** print ads, digital marketing
- **Email marketing:** paid email marketing software, development of email template
- **Networking:** conference fees, travel
- **Promotional materials:** business cards, brochures, fliers, billboards
- **Signage:** wayfinding and studio signage
- **Social media:** management software, dedicated social media intern, paid ads
- **Website:** domain name, hosting, paid programmer/web designer, website builder.

There are free alternatives to many of these tactics. You may be able to use existing web platforms and/or domains, leverage institutional advertising, or get a featured story about your group. You could partner with people already doing social media and ask them to assist with your efforts. If your college has a print center, they could create signage for you at reduced or no cost. You never know until you ask!

Backing up your work

One of the best investments you can make is creating a backup system for your work. Most studios use an online backup or a server. If you use a local server, back it up in the cloud. One time, Meaghan was headed into their student-run studio and heard the fire alarm go off. She grabbed their server and ran outside with it while calling the university police to see if there was a reported fire. It turned out it was just a drill, but from that day forward, she made sure they had a backup of their backup.

In addition to making sure you have backups, organize them logically so that someone unfamiliar with the project can still navigate the files. Create a system for everything—from folder structure, to naming conventions, to how you organize file layers. We recommend creating a folder for each client project that includes project-specific sub-folders. Include archives of any client presentations and date them. Such as a YEAR_MONTH-DAY NAME convention (e.g., 2025_06-18 Client Project.pdf). Include final process work, project documentation, and team photos as well.

Conclusion

For many creatives, the "business" side of design is a challenge. If you're struggling with the fiscal and management sides of design and think you might want to run your own business someday, you might consider taking a studio-management or finance course. But if you've got short-term financial questions, don't hesitate to ask for help! It's okay not to know all the answers at first—no one does!

Also, if you're just starting to charge clients and manage studio expenses, know that it's okay to start small. Sometimes, you get lucky and can start a studio with a lot of funding—but more than likely, you'll be building your business slowly. You'll definitely have a bit of trial and error as you figure out the pacing of projects and how many projects your team can handle in a term.

Chapter 11 key concepts

spec work: unpaid work produced "speculatively" without assurance of eventual payment; often in the form of competitions

sponsored research: projects/research funded by an external company or organization

vendor: an external person or company paid for a service, e.g., illustrator, printer, photographer, programmer

References

1. AIGA. n.d. "Standard Form of Agreement for Design Services." aiga.org/sites/default/files/2021-04/standard-form-of-agreement-for-design-services.pdf.

2. Armstrong, Helen. n.d. "Autonomous Vehicles as Mobile Data Collection Devices." Helen Armstrong. helenarmstrong.info/autonomous-vehicles-as-mobile-data-collection-devices.

AFFINITY DIAGRAMMING

Students create an affinity diagram in preparation for a project in Sarah Rutherford's Graphic Design for Social and Cultural Contexts class at Cleveland State University.

Chapter 12

Planning for the future

Even if you're not planning any significant changes with the studio, you still need a longer-term vision for its future evolution. This includes thinking about how you'll respond to broader cultural and societal conditions, such as social movements for justice and climate change. We also dive into the emerging world of AI and what it might mean for designers doing client work. Be prepared for the fact that you can't do everything right from the start, and things will evolve.

This chapter addresses the challenges and best practices of studio operations when taking over an existing studio and pivoting directions with your current studio. Based on interviews and case studies, we outline best- and worst-case scenarios. We discuss how to handle the handoff between firms, turning repositioning into a design project, and collaborating with other firms within an institution.

HOW? WHO? WHAT? WHY?

> *The best thing that ever happened to me while running these studios was that I got the flu. [This was in 2016, pre-COVID.] I was out for three weeks, and they carried on without me.*
>
> *Since then, I have let go of the reins. Students do it all from start to finish. I provide support and critique. This is hard for first-timers, but by the time they've gone through the studio three times, they are not design students anymore. They are truly junior designers with confidence, art direction, project management, and leadership skills.*

—Amy Johnson, formerly Director of the School of Design and Inktank Studio at the University of Central Oklahoma; currently Professor of Practice, Kansas State University, Department of Interior Architecture and Industrial Design

I (Meaghan) first took over our student-run design studio after the previous director fell in love and eloped. Between the time her contract ended and I started, all of the clients had been left hanging for about two months (while the university was searching for a new director). I tried to pick up the pieces, but I was missing tons of information such as passwords and login information for our studio management tools. We had one very large ($40,000!) client who was very frustrated, and I spent my first few months bending over backward to make them happy (taking calls and meetings after hours). Additionally, their contract was fairly open-ended, so the students and I were constantly doing small design "add-ons" for the client. I also struggled because we didn't have too many other clients, so I had to build a base from scratch. Make your own studio transition a better one than mine!

Transitioning management

After three years running Virginia Tech's student-run studio (FourDesign), I (Meaghan) transitioned into Chair of Graphic Design and a tenure-track position. Once we knew I would be switching positions, we searched for a new director of FourDesign. We set their hiring date to be a few weeks earlier than usual, and I had a brief summer contract to train the new hire. Having several weeks in August before the students came back to campus allowed the new director, Jeff Joiner, to get his feet wet before juggling teaching and other responsibilities.

I would occasionally sit in on meetings, but as Jeff became more comfortable, I handed over the reins. In all honesty, I struggled with letting go as Studio Director. I'd spent years pouring time and energy into the studio and building its reputation, so it was hard to watch someone else take over and do things in their own way. However, each individual brings different strengths into the program, and for instance, Jeff had an advertising background and was able to give his students industry experience and showcase his art direction skills.

Additionally, I helped the transition by attending a few client meetings and classes. We had a new and exciting beer label packaging project for a local brewery, The River Company Restaurant & Brewery—a client I'd connected with a few months earlier. Jeff and I attended initial site/client visits together, and together, we wrote the estimate and worked with our school's business manager to get the contract in the university system. In the following months,

FOURDESIGN

Beer label design for local brewery The River Company Restaurant & Brewery, created by FourDesign.

How to take over a studio

If you are taking over a studio, your approach might be different from the director that came before you. And that's okay! While you might begin by following the processes of your predecessor, you will quickly learn what works well for you and your team (and what doesn't). Maybe you want more client feedback, and you create a client survey. Or perhaps you want more (or fewer) meetings with the students. Additionally, if your specialization differs from your predecessor's, then the specialization offerings of the studio might shift. For example, if you are a motion graphics wizard or a coding queen, perhaps these are services the studio could start offering and advertising.

As we mentioned, we hope you will have a period of transition with the old manager so you can learn the ropes, but this might not be possible. In this case, don't be afraid to lean on other supports such as other faculty members, your department chair, or studio directors at other institutions. (Quite frankly, we think there should be a support group for studio managers!) Regardless of whether or not you have a training period, we recommend having regular meetings (at least twice per year) with all stakeholders—such as business managers/financial supports, administrators, and program chairs—and more frequent check-ins with other faculty/program chairs.

At the larger stakeholder check-in, we recommend that you:
- review the budget (expenses, payments)
- provide a status update on all clients (finished, current, upcoming)
- share goals for the upcoming term
- ask for any assistance that might be needed (e.g., setting up a server).

At the smaller faculty check-in, we recommend that you:
- get feedback for students
- share client successes (and failures)
- ask for any assistance that might be needed (e.g., another faculty member sitting in on a difficult client meeting).

The first year of running a studio is the hardest. You're often forming new relationships in your community, getting the hang of procedures and department politics, and building trust with your students. While studio management is never easy (nothing with clients is!), it gets simpler as you gain confidence and knowledge.

Re-launching a studio

Your faculty manager took a new job, quit, or retired. Your lease ran out on your space. Your university is restructured. There are all sorts of reasons why a studio might fold or "take a pause." At Virginia Tech, we chose to freeze our studio when the director's wife got a job opportunity she couldn't refuse and they moved to Texas with only a few months' notice. Two of our core faculty members were also due to have babies the summer of his departure and were scheduled to be on parental leave the following year—and we didn't have the capacity to hire, train, and oversee a new studio director. While we didn't like taking away an experiential learning opportunity from our students, we also viewed this as a time to reflect on what was working (and what wasn't) and to decide if there was anything we'd like to do differently.

A few of the structural changes we considered were:
- **Space.** Should we keep operating out of a university building, or should we use that as a classroom space and try to rent a facility downtown to be more public-facing?
- **Financial.** What is a reasonable profit goal for the studio? What expenses are necessary, and what can be cut?
- **Scope.** Do we want to keep our focus on graphic design? Do we want to expand to offer additional services, such as AR/VR, advertising, or copywriting?
- **Oversight.** Should we build checkpoints for the organization (such as monthly meetings with the school director, business manager, and program chair)?
- **Structure.** Should the studio continue primarily working with paying clients, or should we pivot to a sponsored research model or try creating more long-term community partnerships?
- **Faculty involvement.** Do we continue to have one studio director, or do we share responsibilities among the design faculty, such as rotating who teaches the studio each semester? If we continue to have one primary director, are there other ways faculty can be involved, such as periodic critiques or assessments?

Freezing a studio has risks—for instance, the studio might never reopen—but sometimes this pause is necessary or unavoidable. And while the relaunch is a lot of work, it's also a chance to rebuild while considering all the lessons you have learned. Additionally, you can address contemporary issues in the core values of your studio relaunch.

Adapting to changing conditions

Planning for the future also includes thinking about how broader societal conditions will shift and affect how we design and create things, interact with each other, and do business. We can't predict the future, but we can try to understand larger trends and prepare ourselves for how we might adapt to long-term and sudden changes. **A good designer knows more than just how to make something look good; they are also aware of what's happening in the world around us and how those conditions and contexts will change how we think about design problems and solutions.** Any designer who works for more than a couple of years will always have to adapt to new technologies, changing economic conditions, and their own evolving interests.

SOCIAL JUSTICE

As designers, we should strive to develop a deep understanding of people and the contexts of their lives. This understanding includes inequitable conditions and increasing disparities across many social indicators, including income, education, and health. Bias and discrimination impact people along many identity markers, including ethnicity, religion, gender, class, ability, and sexual orientation. Younger people—Millennials and Generation Z—are more inclined to take action in response to these systems of oppression.[1] We can expect this trend to continue in the face of increasing cultural conflicts and battles for political power in many countries.

In the field of design, people have developed collectives, organizations, events, and resources to help designers tackle these issues and incorporate them into their work. (See the table below for a list of organizations and resources focusing on design and social justice.)

SOCIAL JUSTICE ORGANIZATIONS AND RESOURCES

ORGANIZATIONS + COMMUNITIES	RESOURCES
Design Justice Network – designjustice.org	*Racism Untaught* – racismuntaught.com
Design as Protest – dapcollective.com	*Decolonizing Reader* – tinyurl.com/y43sukuu
Creative Reaction Lab – crxlab.org	*BIPOC Design History* – bipocdesignhistory.com
The Disabled List – disabledlist.org	*Microsoft Inclusive Design* – inclusive.microsoft.design
Queer Design Club – queerdesign.club	*IDEO AI Ethics Cards* – ideo.com
Algorithmic Justice League – ajl.org	*Liberatory Design Card Deck* – nationalequityproject.org/tools/liberatory-design-card-deck
Data for Black Lives – d4bl.org	*Decolonizing Design: A Cultural Justice Guidebook* – mitpress.mit.edu

CLIMATE CHANGE

The impacts of climate change also intersect with inequitable social and economic outcomes, and designers are taking tangible action to address the drivers and effects of environmental degradation. Organizations and communities like Climate Designers offer resources, tools, training, and events to help designers learn more about current technologies, terms, and policies to employ climate action practices that effectively communicate the issues and encourage people to take action. See the table below for more organizations, communities, and resources specifically focusing on sustainable design and climate change.

CLIMATE CHANGE ORGANIZATIONS AND RESOURCES

ORGANIZATIONS + COMMUNITIES	RESOURCES
Climate Designers – climatedesigners.org	*Design Sustainably* – designsustainably.eu
Creatives for Climate – creativesforclimate.co	*Sustainable Web Design* – sustainablewebdesign.org
Clean Creatives – cleancreatives.org	*Circular Design Guide* – circulardesignguide.com
Sustainable UX Network – sustainableuxnetwork.com	*Climate Action.tech* – climateaction.tech

TECHNOLOGY

During the course of writing this book, ChatGPT arrived on the scene and changed how we think about creating original, human-made work. Then Adobe launched Firefly, an AI tool for generating new images (along with many other variations like DALL-E and Midjourney). Artists and illustrators are pushing back against these tools, raising legal and ethical questions about copyright infringement. In response, Shutterstock announced it would reimburse artists whose images were sold to AI companies. Getty Images promises that its generative AI model is trained only on images found in Getty's own image library.

These developments also raise the question, why spend time working on something if AI can make a better solution—whether it's an illustration, an essay, or a piece of code—much faster than we can? When we really started to freak out about this, we asked ChatGPT to write something for this book (see our Q&A with ChatGPT on the next page).

OUR QUESTION: WHAT IS THE VALUE OF A DESIGNER WHEN AI CAN GENERATE EXCELLENT, FREE DESIGN FAR MORE QUICKLY?

ChatGPT's response

While AI has made significant advancements in generating designs, there is still considerable value in human designers. Here are a few reasons why:

Creativity and innovation: Designers possess a unique ability to think creatively and come up with novel ideas. They can push the boundaries of design, incorporating artistic elements, emotional appeal, and human-centric thinking. AI, on the other hand, relies on pre-existing data and patterns, which limits its ability to generate truly innovative and original designs.

Understanding of context: Designers excel at understanding the specific context, purpose, and audience for a design project. They can consider various factors such as brand identity, user experience, cultural nuances, and aesthetics. This contextual understanding allows designers to create designs that resonate with users on a deeper level, something that AI might struggle with.

Problem solving and adaptability: Design is not just about aesthetics; it's also about problem-solving. Designers are skilled at identifying and solving design challenges, adapting their approach based on feedback and evolving project requirements. They can engage in iterative processes, refining and iterating designs until they meet the desired objectives. AI, although efficient at generating designs, may lack the adaptability and problem-solving capabilities that human designers possess.

Emotional and ethical considerations: Designers are attuned to human emotions and can create designs that evoke specific feelings or responses. They can empathize with users and design interfaces that are intuitive and user-friendly. Additionally, designers can consider ethical implications, ensuring that designs are inclusive, accessible, and align with societal values. AI may not be able to fully comprehend or incorporate these emotional and ethical aspects into its designs.

Collaboration and communication: Design projects often involve collaboration with various stakeholders, such as clients, developers, marketers, and users. Designers are skilled at facilitating communication, understanding requirements, and translating ideas into tangible designs. Their ability to collaborate and work effectively within teams is valuable in the design process.

While AI can assist designers by automating certain repetitive tasks or generating design variations, it is currently considered a tool to enhance human creativity rather than replace it entirely. The combination of AI and human expertise can lead to more powerful and effective design solutions.

Thanks, ChatGPT! That's actually some pretty solid advice! Here's a similar perspective, in our own words:

Clients and community partners will continue to need designers to take a human-centered approach to design challenges and to frame design problems. In the future, the work of designers will likely shift more to the front end of design processes. This shift will require the skills discussed throughout this book—collaboration across disciplines, communication with diverse people and communities, and willingness to learn new concepts, perspectives, and technologies. Even when we use AI tools to help generate imagery, designers will need to develop prompts and iterations to refine concepts and make them suitable for each unique client's needs.

But seriously, what's a designer to do? Well, many people are deeply thinking about how the design profession will change with current and future developments in AI and machine learning. In a podcast interview, Andreas Markdalen, Global Chief Creative Officer at Frog, a design consultancy, recently spoke about these issues. He described how AI could reshape design and creativity in positive ways. He described how designing a brand system for a client could look different when working with emerging and future AI models. Ten years ago, the design team would have developed principles and built a core identity and foundation for the brand, which gets communicated through a brand guideline everyone can use. But now, Andreas thinks that "we're going to see our designers … start to put that input and that learning into specific AI models instead. So that it becomes a kind of engine for creation, where this AI model can help you to generate content, creative ideas, and expression in real-time. It becomes a kind of design tool in that sense in keeping some of these expressions on brand."

Andreas also spoke about the potential for creating digital replicas of yourself and training your own AI models to replicate and automate methodology. He said, "In some sense [this] takes us to this new era of synthetic creativity or synthetic design, where we're starting to kind of co-create things with these specific AI models, and using them as an engine to bring new types of expression to markets."[2] In other words, **something new is taking shape; we're not sure how, but it has the potential to generate new kinds of creativity in the near future that we can't yet imagine.** For now, it is already allowing designers to create complex images and worldmaking that previously required extensive programming and coding knowledge. This opens up opportunities in gaming, virtual reality, and video and film production.

While attending an international conference for Motion Design Educators (MODE), Meaghan participated in an AI discussion group about teaching along with the well-known researcher, Hugh Dubberly. He described people using AI and the phase of, "Oh my god, this is kind of cool" and their transition to, "Oh my god, this is frightening." Our group talked a good deal about how the role of the designer will change. Design educator Kacey Morrow phrased it as, "Rather than honing craft with the pencil, now you're the wizard." We also discussed how students and designers should be transparent with their use of AI, and how documenting process work is even more important. In her use of AI, Meaghan always begins by taking time to ideate before using AI tools—and much like using stock photography, she would rarely use AI-generated content without some revision or customization.

One fear we have about AI is the reduction of entry-level design/illustration/copywriting positions. While (currently) experienced professionals can generally outperform AI, those still developing skills may be discouraged by how well AI can execute tasks. However, **the educational environment can serve as a space for students to be encouraged and provided time to hone their craft.**

Conclusion

This chapter described how to hand over, take over, or re-launch a student-run, faculty-advised studio. We highlighted immediate action items and questions you can ask as you focus and plan for the present and future. Depending on the clients, students, and instructors, dynamics will change from semester to semester.

As you develop your strategies, you'll also need to prepare to continually adapt and respond to changing conditions such as social justice issues, climate change, and technology. **How we think about production and the materiality of design will change. Still, the need to collaborate with real people and real projects probably won't change in our lifetimes.** (We assume AI robots won't completely replace us in the next few years.) The key ideas outlined in this book will always be relevant to your career as a designer—how to collaborate, communicate, reflect, and grow your skills through actual design experience with real-world clients.

Chapter 12 key concepts

artificial intelligence: software systems based on neural networks to make intelligent computer programs

climate change: long-term global shifts in temperatures and weather patterns

social justice: efforts to attain equal rights and equitable opportunities for everyone

References

1. Carnegie, Megan. 2022. "Gen Z: How Young People Are Changing Activism." BBC Worklife. August 8, 2022. bbc.com/worklife/article/20220803-gen-z-how-young-people-are-changing-activism.
2. Design Mind frogcast. n.d. "Human Creativity Meets Creative AI." Accessed June 9, 2023. frog.co/design-mind/design-mind-frogcast-ep-29-human-creativity-meets-creative-ai.

When Jessica gets overwhelmed by the amount of tasks in a giant project, she remembers the advice Anne Lamott describes in her book Bird by Bird. When she was a child, Anne's brother became immobilized by the work of creating a report on birds that he had put off until the last minute. Anne writes, "Then my father sat down beside him, put his arm around my brother's shoulder, and said, 'Bird by bird, buddy. Just take it bird by bird.'"

Conclusion

Self-care & sustainability

Phew, that was a lot of information! We hope you've enjoyed this journey through exploring how to work with design clients in the university classroom. We passionately believe these experiential education interactions are critical to helping young designers develop their skills and knowledge, both personally and professionally. And in case it all seems a little overwhelming right now, we want to distill all of this into two simple proclamations:

It's worth it!
You can do it!

Self-care and sustainability

A faculty member we surveyed said, "Be sure you account for how much time it takes to do this. The demand on faculty time is more than in a regular class." Administrators, particularly those outside the design industry, will likely not understand how much time and effort it takes to run a studio. Additionally, courses dedicated to client work generally create more work for students than a typical class. As such, it's important to utilize good time management strategies and have a support network.

Tips for time management

Break large projects into bite-sized chunks with due dates. If you have a large client project that includes a lot of research and multiple deliverables, don't just put the final due date on the calendar. Rather, figure out week by week what you need to achieve in order to stay on target. For example:
- Week one: conduct user interviews
- Week two: complete affinity diagramming
- Week three: develop personas
- Week four: create and test journey maps
- Week five: create mood boards and initial interface ideas.

Try a weekly check-in. At the start of your week, set aside twenty minutes to write out everything on your to-do list. Include deadlines. Figure out what is most important and what needs to completed first. Try not to avoid larger projects just because something else is easier to finish. Then, look at your week and block off time to complete your work.

Create space for project and midterm feedback. How is a project (or a term) going? Don't wait until a client meeting to find out. Set dates for project reviews. If you're the project leader, try making midterm or mid-project surveys to get a pulse check on how your team is feeling.

Tips for finding emotional and community support

Emotional. Working with clients is hard work. So is juggling multiple classes and projects. And sometimes things don't go how you wanted—a client hates your design solution, a team member quits, or something goes wrong in your personal life. Having some support in place *before things go wrong* can really help. While friends and family can be good supports, don't be afraid to reach out to a therapist or counselor if you feel you need extra assistance. Many institutions even offer free counseling services.

Administrative. When you have multiple fires to put out with your client work, it helps to know you can count on the support of your faculty or administrators. The responsibilities of projects or studios shouldn't fall solely on the shoulders of students or one faculty member. But this also means if something is going wrong and you don't have the resources to handle it, you should communicate this to others. It's easy to want to look like you have everything under control (even when you don't), but a part of long-term success is knowing when to ask for assistance.

Community. Ideally, you have a positive "studio culture" at your institution, meaning that students, faculty, and community members have an inclusive and inspiring work environment. They also care about design beyond the classroom. People might get together for other activities like hosting visiting designers, watching design films and shows, having reading and discussion groups, or studio time working together in the same space, and sometimes giving each other feedback. If this is not the case at your school, you can look elsewhere for the community connection. Look for local design organizations or connect with others online. You could also build a partnership with another institution through which students can get feedback from one another. A goal of connecting with a broader network is to stay inspired and excited about design and to be aware of current industry practices.

Mentorship. As we discuss at greater length in *Chapter 3*, by giving and receiving mentorship, people learn about equitable power sharing and successful collaborations. A mentor can also be a person to bounce ideas off of, learn from, and occasionally vent to. Hopefully, you have a mentor at your institution, but you might also find mentors at other institutions or within the industry. The best mentoring relationships evolve somewhat organically and aren't forced. Perhaps you saw someone give a presentation that resonated with you, and you struck up a conversation. Or maybe you attended a conference or event and discovered your mutual interests. These mentoring relationships might be set up more formally (e.g., a scheduled once-a-month meeting, official title as "mentor" and "mentee"), or less so (e.g., the occasional lunch or phone call). Regardless, these are most successful when they feel mutually beneficial. Even if you are the mentee, you still have much to offer, such as a fresh perspective and insights about challenges and opportunities.

Burnout and recharging

Even if you have strategies and support in place, you might find yourself burning out. Burnout refers to feeling physically, emotionally, or mentally exhausted—usually due to prolonged stress. Whether you are an ambitious student or trying to jumpstart your career, it's easy to burn the candle at both ends.

In *Designing Design*, Kenya Hara writes that "the mind exists everywhere in the body."[1] This reminds us that, while we often speak about mental and physical health separately, the two are actually intertwined. Sleeping, eating well, and getting moving will all positively contribute to both your mental health and your intellectual abilities. While it's difficult (if not impossible) to always do well at school and work, get a good night's sleep, cook healthy foods, and still find time to hit the gym and hang out with friends and family, finding balance will help you from burning out. Some people strive to make space for each of these areas for a day or a week, but it's also okay to prioritize different areas from week to week—such as knocking out a big project before you enjoy a vacation.

Connecting to nature—going for a walk outdoors or sitting in sunlight—can also help with recharging. One of our favorite internet memes is someone saying they were starting to feel depressed, but then they spent the afternoon outdoors on a sunny day and felt better. They joke, "It turns out I'm just a complicated plant." Over time, you will find strategies that work for you (and try to remember what works!). Treating yourself by taking a long bath, meeting friends for brunch, or spending an evening curled up watching a movie is okay.

But inward-facing care is only one strategy. You can also reach outward. Emily Nagoski, author of *Burnout: The Secret To Unlocking The Stress Cycle*, says, "The cure for burnout is not self-care. It's all of us caring for each other."[2] Building a community of support and turning to each other can keep us connected and in good balance with all parts of ourselves.

CONCLUSION 215

Empowerment

It makes sense that we end this book focusing on self-care and community, which brings us back to personal and intellectual growth through experiential learning. We hope that as you continue in your education and career, you achieve a sense of empowerment. We hope you forge a self-directed path by reflecting on your sense of purpose and developing a sense of agency. We hope you find a meaningful role in society through mentoring and educational experiences, combined with engagement with clients and communities.

In your own words

But who are we to say? We're just professors. We'll end here (on the following spreads) with words from your peers—our students—who have taken part in experiential client work in the design classroom.

References

1. Hara, Kenya. 2018. *Designing Design*. Lars Müller Publishers.
2. Nagoski, Amelia and Nagoski, Emily. 2019. *Burnout: The Secret to Unlocking the Stress Cycle*. Ballantine Books.

What did you learn while working with clients or community partners that you didn't learn in a traditional design studio class?

How to deal with subjective opinions from non-designers.

Molly Vinson Piersol
Virginia Tech (FourDesign) alum

Storytelling as presentation, how conflict can be productive, how to manage clients or project managers with strong opinions.

Casey Davis
Virginia Tech (FourDesign) alum

I got my first look at working with real world clients and adhering to requests and being flexible with what different clients want, while also working to the standards of the studio. I think what's different from learning in Design Streak than in a traditional class, is that traditional classes don't show how hectic being a designer or being in the studio can be.

Tony Williams
Illinois State University (Design Streak) alum

CONCLUSION 217

> Design sounds like a really monolithic thing if you don't have experience in the field. Most people just assume it's graphic design and making things look pretty. But when you dive in, you see design is a blend of art, science, business strategy, and sometimes engineering. It's an incredibly diverse discipline and has arguably never been more valuable in the world than it is right now.
>
> Brett Simone
> Virginia Tech (PRISM) alum

What was the most valuable part of this experience for you?

> Learning how to communicate with clients was the most valuable takeaway. I learned how to ask questions, articulate a vision, and ultimately sell clients on my work. This gave me a greater sense of confidence upon graduating and ultimately is what lead me to open my own business one year later.
>
> Micah Vetter
> Illinois State University (Design Streak) alum

> Learning how to speak to clients respectfully while still getting them over to your side and to trust you.
>
> Molly Vinson Piersol
> Virginia Tech (FourDesign) alum

> At first, say yes to everything. Soak up all the experience you can, both good and bad, you'll learn from both. Then, as you gain experience, do everything you can to find like-minded clients. Get comfortable saying no if you don't feel you see eye to eye with a partner. Nothing is worse than working for a client who doesn't understand your value or how to unleash it.
>
> Brett Simone
> Virginia Tech (PRISM) alum

Do you have any advice for current students who will be working with clients and community partners?

> You must be flexible and able to work around the clients.
>
> Tony Williams
> Illinois State University (Design Streak) alum

> It is always best to have an attitude of humility. Instead of assuming you know best, ask others for their opinions. When meeting with clients or community partners, ask about their experience. Find what they need and fill it. When you solve other people's problems, you make the world a better place and also leave a positive impression that could help you out in the future.
>
> Micah Vetter
> Illinois State University (Design Streak) alum

Do you feel that working with clients in the classroom helped prepare you for your current job? Why or why not?

Absolutely. Working with clients in the university classroom increased the maturity level with which I treated my work. It gave me a larger world view and made me realize the importance of design. Working with real clients gave me the determination to make excellent work. This attitude has spilled into my current job and is most likely the reason my business has grown as quickly as it has.

Micah Vetter
Illinois State University
(Design Streak) alum

Yes because I had a leg-up on others who were sometimes shocked by clients' responses and wouldn't know how to solve problems because of it. I understood more quickly what the client was actually asking for or why they didn't like something.

Molly Vinson Piersol
Virginia Tech
(FourDesign) alum

100%. The vast majority of my classes as a marketing student focused on market research, sales, and a little brand management. My learning curve in advertising as a creative would've been much steeper without doing this work first. It was a critical bridge between what I learned in class and what I needed to do in the business world.

Brett Simone
Virginia Tech (PRISM) alum

Index

NOTE

Page locators in italic refer to figure captions

A

accrediting bodies 39
advertising 91, 196
advertising agency roles 120
agency 46, 54, 58
AIGA 8, 29, 36, 38, 83, 84, 122, *123*
alumni relationships 29
applying for client-based programs 127
apprenticeships 48
Armstrong, Helen 191, 192–5
Arsaga's Coffee 130–3
art directors 120, 122, *123*, 129
artificial intelligence (AI) 205, 206, 207, 209
assessment 102, 109
attention to detail 154
auto-ethnography 25
typographic timeline 22, 23, *112*

B

backing up work 196
beginning work 146
Belbin Team Roles 117
Benbrahim, Dina 130–3
best practices for design programs 36–8
brainstorming 70
budgets 180, 181
burnout 214

C

care, communicating 21
careers 52, 121
case studies 130–3, 192–5
change, adapting to 204–7
ChatGPT 205, 206
civic partnerships 31
clients
    to charge or not to charge 89–90, 182–3
    choosing client partnerships 185
    developing relationships 141
    establishing relationships 135–51
    external 88, 136, 183, 185
    feedback 141, 142–3
    finding 56, 90–1, 92, 174
    initial meetings 136–7
    internal 88, 91, 136, 183, 185
    services to offer 86–8
    support from 158
    sustaining relationships 153–9
    types 88–90
    understanding 136–7
    when to say "no" to 156
Clifton-Strengths 117
climate change 205, 209
clubs and organizations 29
co-creation 68–9, *69*, 79
codes of conduct 73, 124
codes of ethics 72, 73
communities, engaging with 63–81
community
    agreements 124, *125*, 129
    engagement as empowering 47, 48, 54
    outreach offices 31
    principles of 124
    role of studio in 172
    of support 213, 214
community partners 91, 92, 183
    building relationships with 31, 32–3
    connecting to industry and 27–41
    models for engagement 28–9
    support from 158
compensation 88–9, 182, 184
competitions 29, 187
contracts 187, 188
core values, focus on 166
creative briefs 30, 138–9, 151
critique and reflection 106–7
curricular models, comparing 101–5
curricular structure 101

D

Dermody, Brenda 92–3
design, defining 16

design firms and agencies 28
    roles in 123
Design Sprint methodology 149
Design Streak 8, 56–7
design with not for 64
designExplorr 62, 75, 76–7
DesignUP 10, 14, 78, 80–1, 96, 115, 152, 184
DesignWorks process 145, 146, 147
disagreements, dealing with 124
donations 90, 182
DPC weekly progress rubric 104

E

emotional support 213, 214
empathy 67, 79
empowerment 43–59, 93, 215
    catalysts of 44, 46–52
    defining 58
    model for 22, 44–5, 44
    professional identity development 52–5
    in youth 44–5
equitable practices 32, 68–71, 93, 175
equity 24, 25
estimates 186
ethics 24, 25, 72–4, 155
expenses 180, 181, 188, 196
external clients 88, 136, 183, 185

F

fee-for-service 89, 95
feedback
    client 141, 142–3
    and reflection 106–7
Finley, Patrick 78, 80–1
fiscal support 182
focus, finding 86–8, 165
FourDesign 94, 118–19, 164, 173, 201
FourSight model 117
framing 122, 129
future, planning for 199–209

G

group review 104

H

hourly rate, charging 189, 190

I

inclusive design 69–71
industry
    connecting to community and 27–41
    models for engagement with 28–9
    standards 36–8
    support from partners in 158
instructors, roles for 122
intakes 146, 151
intellectual property rights 187
internal clients 88, 91, 136, 183, 185
international collaborations 75
International Society of Typographic Designers (ISTD) 29
    example brief 30
internships 20, 40
intersectionality 66, 67, 79
interviewing for client-based programs 127
interviews 32–3, 56–7, 76–7, 80–1, 92–3, 133, 174–5
invoices 189

L

Laker, Penina 21, 31, 32–3, 34
laws and regulations 170
lead times 145, 147, 148, 151
leadership roles 116
learning goals, achieving 97–109
learning outcomes 39–40, 41
    defining course- and program-level 100
    establishing standards and 36–8
    examples 39, 40, 94, 174
learning through doing 18

Index, continued

learning through experience 20–1, 46–7, 53, 114
   advice from educators 34–5
   empowerment and 51
   students on 215–19
learning together 99
licensing agreements 189
listening and communicating across difference 68
local organizations and agencies 75, 170

M

market position 170, 177
marketing 196
mentoring 47, 48, 54, 56–7, 122, 213
metacognition 19, 25
milestones 137, 144, 151
Mint Design Studio 39, 169, 174–5, 185
mission statements 94, 168–9
monetary services 89, 90, 182, 183, 185
money management 179–97
multisensory design 69–71

N

name, studio 170, 171
NASAD 39
national collaborations 75
needs, identifying 167
networking 31, 91
non-disclosure agreements (NDAs) 187
non-monetary services 89, 90, 182, 183, 185
nonprofit organizations 31, 80–1, 88, 185
nonprofit structure 183

O

The One Club 29
others, understanding 65

P

participatory design 69
peer review 104

practicum 18, 20, 25
praxis 72, 79
principles of community 124
problem-solving by design 16–17
professional code of conduct 73
professional identity development 52–5
professionalism 126, 129
project briefs 140
project management 145–7
purpose of student-run agencies 165

R

re-launching studios 203
recharging 214
reciprocal relationships 75, 90, 95
Red Hat 192–5
referrals 91
reflection 19, 47, 53
   and critique 106–7
requests for proposals (RFP) 91, 95
Rogal, Maria 35, 174–5
rubrics 103, 104, 109

S

scales, collaborating at different 75
scheduling and coordination 148
scope of work 137, 146, 151
   framing 86–8
self-care and sustainability 211–15
self-reflection 47, 64, 65, 105
sense of purpose 46, 47, 54, 58
services and specializations 86–8, 165
Shekara, Archana 35, 56–7
skills, developing design 84–5
Slone, Ryan 34, 130–3
SMART goal planning 144
Social Change Map 117
social contracts 124, 125, 129
social enterprises 75, 76–7
social justice 204, 209
social media 91, 120, 196
spec work 187, 197

sponsored research 28, 41, 191
    Red Hat 192–5
stakeholders 159
support from 157–8
standards 36–8
student roles 114–21
studios
    in community 172
    in curriculum 172
    finding a space 173
    internally funded model 190
    launching 163–77
    naming 170, 171
    pausing and re-launching 203
    "personality" 171
    purpose 165
    roles 118–19
    taking over 202
    transitioning management 201
Superpowers (SYPartners) 54, 55
support
    finding emotional and community 213, 214
    fiscal 182
    from stakeholders 157–8
sustainable development goals 54, 55
SWOT analysis 166, 177
syllabus statements 21
systemic issues 32, 41

T

team roles 116–17
Technological University, Dublin 92–3
technology 205–7
time management 149, 212
time recording 190
timelines, setting 145, 147, 148
transition to adulthood
    catalysts of empowerment 44, 46–52
    developing professional identity 52–5
    model of integrated
        empowerment in 22, 44–5, 44

Type Directors Club 29
typographic timelines 22, 23, 112

U

University of Arkansas School of Art 130–3

V

value, articulating 157
value propositions 171, 177
vendors, working with 188, 197
vision statements 168–9

W

Walker, Jacinda 42, 62, 75, 76–7
work roles 113–29

Image credits

Every effort has been made to trace, clear, and credit the appropriate copyright holders of the images reproduced in this book. However, if any credits have been inadvertently omitted or in error, the publisher will incorporate amendments in future printings. All diagrams and illustrations were created by the authors unless otherwise noted.

Introduction
pp. 4, 5 Photos of students (courtesy of Patrick Finley)
p. 5 Photography scene (courtesy of Donna Wertalik)
p. 6 Photo of Design Streak Studio (courtesy of Archana Shekara, photo by Lyndsie Schlick)
p. 10 Photo of students working (courtesy of Patrick Finley)

Chapter 1
p. 14 Photo of DesignUP (courtesy of Patrick Finley)
p. 17 Illustration based on "Woman Teacher Working With Female College Students In Library" (photo by Monkey Business Images, Dissolve Premium)
pp. 22, 23 Photos of "Auto-ethnography Typographic Timeline" (courtesy of Renée Walker)

Chapter 2
p. 26 Students build gallery installation (courtesy of Sarah Rutherford)
p. 30 Beata Sarkadi work (courtesy of Brenda Dermody)
p. 31 Photo of students working (courtesy of Penina Laker)
p. 32 Penina Laker headshot (courtesy of Penina Laker)
p. 37 Student work examples (courtesy of Penina Laker)
p. 38 AIGA Design Futures Trends (courtesy of AIGA)

Chapter 3
p. 42 Photo of Spark216 (courtesy of Jacinda Walker)
p. 49 Illustration based on "Smiling People Working with Computer" (photo by SeventyFour, iStock by Getty Images, 827502778)
p. 50 Illustration based on "Happy delivery" (photo by Akarawut Lohacharoenvanich, iStock by Getty Images, 1400178233)
pp. 54, 55 Superpowers card deck (SYPartners)
p. 55 Sustainable Development Goals (United Nations, Department of Economic and Social Affairs. https://sdgs.un.org/goals)
p. 56 Archana Shekara headshot (courtesy of Archana Shekara)
p. 57 Photo of Design Streak Studio (courtesy of Archana Shekara, photo by Lyndsie Schlick)

Chapter 4
p. 62 designExplorr workshop (courtesy of Jacinda Walker)
p. 69 *Say, Do, and Make* diagram (courtesy of Elizabeth Sanders and Pieter Jan Stappers, © Sanders & Stappers)
p. 76 Jacinda Walker headshot (courtesy of Jacinda Walker)
p. 77 STEAM Academy (courtesy of Jacinda Walker)
p. 78 Photos of DesignUP (courtesy of Patrick Finley)
p. 80 Patrick Finley headshot (courtesy of Patrick Finley)

Chapter 5
p. 82 Photo of students and fabricators (courtesy of Penina Laker)
p. 84 Photo of PRISM (courtesy of Donna Wertalik)
p. 85 Diagram adapted from Juliette Cezzar's "The AIGA Guide to Careers in Graphic & Communication Design" (courtesy of Juliette Cezzar)
p. 90 Illustration based on "Teacher Proctoring His Students During an Examination" (CC photo by RDNE Stock project, Pexels.com)
p. 92 Brenda Dermody headshot (courtesy of Brenda Dermody)

Chapter 6
p. 96 Photo of DesignUP (courtesy of Patrick Finley)
p. 108 Photo of DesignUP (courtesy of Patrick Finley)

Chapter 7
p. 112 Photo of students working (courtesy of Renée Walker)
p. 115 Photos of DesignUP (courtesy of Patrick Finley)
p. 121 Illustration based on "I just wanted to get someone's opinion on this..." (photo by gettyimages, 484189135)
p. 123 Diagram adapted from Juliette Cezzar's "The AIGA Guide to Careers in Graphic & Communication Design" (courtesy of Juliette Cezzar)
p. 125 Illustration based on "Two students arguing doing homework" (photo by AntonioGuillem, iStock by Getty Images, 953902366)
p. 130 Headshot of Dina Benbrahim (courtesy of Dina Benbrahim)
p. 130 Headshot of Ryan Slone (courtesy of Ryan Slone)
pp. 130, 131, 132, 133 Images of student work and Artsagas (courtesy of Dina Benbrahim and Ryan Slone)

Chapter 8
p. 134 Photo of student photo shoot (courtesy of Donna Wertalik)
p. 140 Student work (courtesy of Annabelle Gould)
p. 149 Diagram of Google's Design Sprint Methodology (based on https://designsprintkit.withgoogle.com/methodology/overview)

Chapter 9
p. 152 Photo of DesignUP (courtsey of Patrick Finley)

Chapter 10
p. 162 Student critique (courtesy of Sarah Rutherford)
p. 164 Illustration based on CCO Happy executives sharing pizza in conference room (photo by pikwizard.com)
p. 173 Student work (courtesy of FourDesign)
p. 174 Maria Rogal headshot (courtsey of Maria Rogal)
p. 174 Mint Design Studio (courtsey of Maria Rogal)

Chapter 11
p. 178 Student at work (courtesy of Helen Armstrong)
p. 184 Swag (courtesy of Helen Armstrong)
p. 185 Students from Mint Design Studio (courtesy of Maria Rogal)
p. 188 Diagram based on AIGA (aiga.org/resources/business-freelance-resources)
p. 192 Helen Armstrong headshot (courtesy of Helen Armstrong)
pp. 192, 193, 194, 195 Red Hat case study images (courtesy of Helen Armstrong)

Chapter 12
p. 198 Students create an affinity diagram (courtesy of Sarah Rutherford)
p. 200 Illustration based on "Nobody understand you better than your bed" (photo by ljubaphoto, iStock by Getty Images, 945264466)
p. 201 Peachicot label design (courtesy of FourDesign)

Conclusion
p. 210 Image generated by Midjourney via a prompt by the authors